ᴚEER EXAMINATION SERIES

THIS IS YOUR **PASSBOOK®** FOR ...

PHYSICIAN'S ASSISTANT

NATIONAL LEARNING CORPORATION®
passbooks.com

COPYRIGHT NOTICE

212 Michael Drive, Syosset, NY 11791
(516) 921-8888 • www.passbooks.com
E-mail: info@passbooks.com

PUBLISHED IN THE UNITED STATES OF AMERICA

PASSBOOK® SERIES

THE *PASSBOOK® SERIES* has been created to prepare applicants and candidates for the ultimate academic battlefield – the examination room.

At some time in our lives, each and every one of us may be required to take an examination – for validation, matriculation, admission, qualification, registration, certification, or licensure.

Based on the assumption that every applicant or candidate has met the basic formal educational standards, has taken the required number of courses, and read the necessary texts, the *PASSBOOK® SERIES* furnishes the one special preparation which may assure passing with confidence, instead of failing with insecurity. Examination questions – together with answers – are furnished as the basic vehicle for study so that the mysteries of the examination and its compounding difficulties may be eliminated or diminished by a sure method.

This book is meant to help you pass your examination provided that you qualify and are serious in your objective.

The entire field is reviewed through the huge store of content information which is succinctly presented through a provocative and challenging approach – the question-and-answer method.

A climate of success is established by furnishing the correct answers at the end of each test.

You soon learn to recognize types of questions, forms of questions, and patterns of questioning. You may even begin to anticipate expected outcomes.

You perceive that many questions are repeated or adapted so that you can gain acute insights, which may enable you to score many sure points.

You learn how to confront new questions, or types of questions, and to attack them confidently and work out the correct answers.

You note objectives and emphases, and recognize pitfalls and dangers, so that you may make positive educational adjustments.

Moreover, you are kept fully informed in relation to new concepts, methods, practices, and directions in the field.

You discover that you arre actually taking the examination all the time: you are preparing for the examination by "taking" an examination, not by reading extraneous and/or supererogatory textbooks.

In short, this PASSBOOK®, used directedly, should be an important factor in helping you to pass your test.

PHYSICIAN'S ASSISTANT

DUTIES AND RESPONSIBILITIES

As a Physician's Assistant, under the supervision of a licensed physician, you would assist the physician in diagnosis and treatment of clients. You would perform routine medical examinations on clients; write prescriptions and submit them to the physician for countersignature; order standard laboratory and x-ray procedures; and evaluate laboratory tests. When necessary, you would refer abnormal findings to the physician; initiate proper treatment for emergency cases; and contact the physician for further assistance. You may also perform employee health examinations; performs related work.

EXAMPLES OF TYPICAL TASKS

Obtains detailed case histories on patients on admission, and compiles and records detailed narrative case summaries; as directed, may perform physical examinations and record and present resulting data to the supervising physician; as directed, may perform such routine procedures as injections, immunizations, and the suturing and care of wounds; assists supervising physician in making patient rounds, recording patient progress notes, and in executing standing orders and other specific orders or procedures at the direction of the supervising physician; assists supervising physician in the delivery of service to patients requiring continuing care, including the review and monitoring of treatment and therapy plans; performs evaluative and treatment procedures essential to provide appropriate response to life-threatening, emergency situations; may perform or assist in the performance of routine laboratory or related procedures.

TESTS

The written test will deal, in whole or part, with the duties and responsibilities, and typical tasks listed above.

HOW TO TAKE A TEST

I. YOU MUST PASS AN EXAMINATION

A. WHAT EVERY CANDIDATE SHOULD KNOW

Examination applicants often ask us for help in preparing for the written test. What can I study in advance? What kinds of questions will be asked? How will the test be given? How will the papers be graded?

As an applicant for a civil service examination, you may be wondering about some of these things. Our purpose here is to suggest effective methods of advance study and to describe civil service examinations.

Your chances for success on this examination can be increased if you know how to prepare. Those "pre-examination jitters" can be reduced if you know what to expect. You can even experience an adventure in good citizenship if you know why civil service exams are given.

B. WHY ARE CIVIL SERVICE EXAMINATIONS GIVEN?

Civil service examinations are important to you in two ways. As a citizen, you want public jobs filled by employees who know how to do their work. As a job seeker, you want a fair chance to compete for that job on an equal footing with other candidates. The best-known means of accomplishing this two-fold goal is the competitive examination.

Exams are widely publicized throughout the nation. They may be administered for jobs in federal, state, city, municipal, town or village governments or agencies.

Any citizen may apply, with some limitations, such as the age or residence of applicants. Your experience and education may be reviewed to see whether you meet the requirements for the particular examination. When these requirements exist, they are reasonable and applied consistently to all applicants. Thus, a competitive examination may cause you some uneasiness now, but it is your privilege and safeguard.

C. HOW ARE CIVIL SERVICE EXAMS DEVELOPED?

Examinations are carefully written by trained technicians who are specialists in the field known as "psychological measurement," in consultation with recognized authorities in the field of work that the test will cover. These experts recommend the subject matter areas or skills to be tested; only those knowledges or skills important to your success on the job are included. The most reliable books and source materials available are used as references. Together, the experts and technicians judge the difficulty level of the questions.

Test technicians know how to phrase questions so that the problem is clearly stated. Their ethics do not permit "trick" or "catch" questions. Questions may have been tried out on sample groups, or subjected to statistical analysis, to determine their usefulness.

Written tests are often used in combination with performance tests, ratings of training and experience, and oral interviews. All of these measures combine to form the best-known means of finding the right person for the right job.

II. HOW TO PASS THE WRITTEN TEST

A. NATURE OF THE EXAMINATION

To prepare intelligently for civil service examinations, you should know how they differ from school examinations you have taken. In school you were assigned certain definite pages to read or subjects to cover. The examination questions were quite detailed and usually emphasized memory. Civil service exams, on the other hand, try to discover your present ability to perform the duties of a position, plus your potentiality to learn these duties. In other words, a civil service exam attempts to predict how successful you will be. Questions cover such a broad area that they cannot be as minute and detailed as school exam questions.

In the public service similar kinds of work, or positions, are grouped together in one "class." This process is known as *position-classification*. All the positions in a class are paid according to the salary range for that class. One class title covers all of these positions, and they are all tested by the same examination.

B. FOUR BASIC STEPS

1) Study the announcement

How, then, can you know what subjects to study? Our best answer is: "Learn as much as possible about the class of positions for which you've applied." The exam will test the knowledge, skills and abilities needed to do the work.

Your most valuable source of information about the position you want is the official exam announcement. This announcement lists the training and experience qualifications. Check these standards and apply only if you come reasonably close to meeting them.

The brief description of the position in the examination announcement offers some clues to the subjects which will be tested. Think about the job itself. Review the duties in your mind. Can you perform them, or are there some in which you are rusty? Fill in the blank spots in your preparation.

Many jurisdictions preview the written test in the exam announcement by including a section called "Knowledge and Abilities Required," "Scope of the Examination," or some similar heading. Here you will find out specifically what fields will be tested.

2) Review your own background

Once you learn in general what the position is all about, and what you need to know to do the work, ask yourself which subjects you already know fairly well and which need improvement. You may wonder whether to concentrate on improving your strong areas or on building some background in your fields of weakness. When the announcement has specified "some knowledge" or "considerable knowledge," or has used adjectives like "beginning principles of..." or "advanced ... methods," you can get a clue as to the number and difficulty of questions to be asked in any given field. More questions, and hence broader coverage, would be included for those subjects which are more important in the work. Now weigh your strengths and weaknesses against the job requirements and prepare accordingly.

3) Determine the level of the position

Another way to tell how intensively you should prepare is to understand the level of the job for which you are applying. Is it the entering level? In other words, is this the position in which beginners in a field of work are hired? Or is it an intermediate or advanced level? Sometimes this is indicated by such words as "Junior" or "Senior" in the class title. Other jurisdictions use Roman numerals to designate the level – Clerk I, Clerk II, for example. The word "Supervisor" sometimes appears in the title. If the level is not indicated by the title, check the description of duties. Will you be working under very close supervision, or will you have responsibility for independent decisions in this work?

4) Choose appropriate study materials

Now that you know the subjects to be examined and the relative amount of each subject to be covered, you can choose suitable study materials. For beginning level jobs, or even advanced ones, if you have a pronounced weakness in some aspect of your training, read a modern, standard textbook in that field. Be sure it is up to date and has general coverage. Such books are normally available at your library, and the librarian will be glad to help you locate one. For entry-level positions, questions of appropriate difficulty are chosen – neither highly advanced questions, nor those too simple. Such questions require careful thought but not advanced training.

If the position for which you are applying is technical or advanced, you will read more advanced, specialized material. If you are already familiar with the basic principles of your field, elementary textbooks would waste your time. Concentrate on advanced textbooks and technical periodicals. Think through the concepts and review difficult problems in your field.

These are all general sources. You can get more ideas on your own initiative, following these leads. For example, training manuals and publications of the government agency which employs workers in your field can be useful, particularly for technical and professional positions. A letter or visit to the government department involved may result in more specific study suggestions, and certainly will provide you with a more definite idea of the exact nature of the position you are seeking.

III. KINDS OF TESTS

Tests are used for purposes other than measuring knowledge and ability to perform specified duties. For some positions, it is equally important to test ability to make adjustments to new situations or to profit from training. In others, basic mental abilities not dependent on information are essential. Questions which test these things may not appear as pertinent to the duties of the position as those which test for knowledge and information. Yet they are often highly important parts of a fair examination. For very general questions, it is almost impossible to help you direct your study efforts. What we can do is to point out some of the more common of these general abilities needed in public service positions and describe some typical questions.

1) General information

Broad, general information has been found useful for predicting job success in some kinds of work. This is tested in a variety of ways, from vocabulary lists to questions about current events. Basic background in some field of work, such as sociology or economics, may be sampled in a group of questions. Often these are principles which have become familiar to most persons through exposure rather than through formal training. It is difficult to advise you how to study for these questions; being alert to the world around you is our best suggestion.

2) Verbal ability

An example of an ability needed in many positions is verbal or language ability. Verbal ability is, in brief, the ability to use and understand words. Vocabulary and grammar tests are typical measures of this ability. Reading comprehension or paragraph interpretation questions are common in many kinds of civil service tests. You are given a paragraph of written material and asked to find its central meaning.

3) Numerical ability

Number skills can be tested by the familiar arithmetic problem, by checking paired lists of numbers to see which are alike and which are different, or by interpreting charts and graphs. In the latter test, a graph may be printed in the test booklet which you are asked to use as the basis for answering questions.

4) Observation

A popular test for law-enforcement positions is the observation test. A picture is shown to you for several minutes, then taken away. Questions about the picture test your ability to observe both details and larger elements.

5) Following directions

In many positions in the public service, the employee must be able to carry out written instructions dependably and accurately. You may be given a chart with several columns, each column listing a variety of information. The questions require you to carry out directions involving the information given in the chart.

6) Skills and aptitudes

Performance tests effectively measure some manual skills and aptitudes. When the skill is one in which you are trained, such as typing or shorthand, you can practice. These tests are often very much like those given in business school or high school courses. For many of the other skills and aptitudes, however, no short-time preparation can be made. Skills and abilities natural to you or that you have developed throughout your lifetime are being tested.

Many of the general questions just described provide all the data needed to answer the questions and ask you to use your reasoning ability to find the answers. Your best preparation for these tests, as well as for tests of facts and ideas, is to be at your physical and mental best. You, no doubt, have your own methods of getting into an exam-taking mood and keeping “in shape.” The next section lists some ideas on this subject.

IV. KINDS OF QUESTIONS

Only rarely is the “essay” question, which you answer in narrative form, used in civil service tests. Civil service tests are usually of the short-answer type. Full instructions for answering these questions will be given to you at the examination. But in case this is your first experience with short-answer questions and separate answer sheets, here is what you need to know:

1) Multiple-choice Questions

Most popular of the short-answer questions is the "multiple choice" or "best answer" question. It can be used, for example, to test for factual knowledge, ability to solve problems or judgment in meeting situations found at work.

A multiple-choice question is normally one of three types—

- It can begin with an incomplete statement followed by several possible endings. You are to find the one ending which *best* completes the statement, although some of the others may not be entirely wrong.
- It can also be a complete statement in the form of a question which is answered by choosing one of the statements listed.
- It can be in the form of a problem – again you select the best answer.

Here is an example of a multiple-choice question with a discussion which should give you some clues as to the method for choosing the right answer:

When an employee has a complaint about his assignment, the action which will *best* help him overcome his difficulty is to

A. discuss his difficulty with his coworkers
B. take the problem to the head of the organization
C. take the problem to the person who gave him the assignment
D. say nothing to anyone about his complaint

In answering this question, you should study each of the choices to find which is best. Consider choice "A" – Certainly an employee may discuss his complaint with fellow employees, but no change or improvement can result, and the complaint remains unresolved. Choice "B" is a poor choice since the head of the organization probably does not know what assignment you have been given, and taking your problem to him is known as "going over the head" of the supervisor. The supervisor, or person who made the assignment, is the person who can clarify it or correct any injustice. Choice "C" is, therefore, correct. To say nothing, as in choice "D," is unwise. Supervisors have and interest in knowing the problems employees are facing, and the employee is seeking a solution to his problem.

2) True/False Questions

The "true/false" or "right/wrong" form of question is sometimes used. Here a complete statement is given. Your job is to decide whether the statement is right or wrong.

SAMPLE: A roaming cell-phone call to a nearby city costs less than a non-roaming call to a distant city.

This statement is wrong, or false, since roaming calls are more expensive.

This is not a complete list of all possible question forms, although most of the others are variations of these common types. You will always get complete directions for answering questions. Be sure you understand *how* to mark your answers – ask questions until you do.

V. RECORDING YOUR ANSWERS

Computer terminals are used more and more today for many different kinds of exams.

For an examination with very few applicants, you may be told to record your answers in the test booklet itself. Separate answer sheets are much more common. If this separate answer sheet is to be scored by machine – and this is often the case – it is highly important that you mark your answers correctly in order to get credit.

An electronic scoring machine is often used in civil service offices because of the speed with which papers can be scored. Machine-scored answer sheets must be marked with a pencil, which will be given to you. This pencil has a high graphite content which responds to the electronic scoring machine. As a matter of fact, stray dots may register as answers, so do not let your pencil rest on the answer sheet while you are pondering the correct answer. Also, if your pencil lead breaks or is otherwise defective, ask for another.

Since the answer sheet will be dropped in a slot in the scoring machine, be careful not to bend the corners or get the paper crumpled.

The answer sheet normally has five vertical columns of numbers, with 30 numbers to a column. These numbers correspond to the question numbers in your test booklet. After each number, going across the page are four or five pairs of dotted lines. These short dotted lines have small letters or numbers above them. The first two pairs may also have a "T" or "F" above the letters. This indicates that the first two pairs only are to be used if the questions are of the true-false type. If the questions are multiple choice, disregard the "T" and "F" and pay attention only to the small letters or numbers.

Answer your questions in the manner of the sample that follows:

32. The largest city in the United States is
    - A. Washington, D.C.
    - B. New York City
    - C. Chicago
    - D. Detroit
    - E. San Francisco

1) Choose the answer you think is best. (New York City is the largest, so "B" is correct.)
2) Find the row of dotted lines numbered the same as the question you are answering. (Find row number 32)
3) Find the pair of dotted lines corresponding to the answer. (Find the pair of lines under the mark "B.")
4) Make a solid black mark between the dotted lines.

VI. BEFORE THE TEST

Common sense will help you find procedures to follow to get ready for an examination. Too many of us, however, overlook these sensible measures. Indeed, nervousness and fatigue have been found to be the most serious reasons why applicants fail to do their best on civil service tests. Here is a list of reminders:

- Begin your preparation early – Don't wait until the last minute to go scurrying around for books and materials or to find out what the position is all about.
- Prepare continuously – An hour a night for a week is better than an all-night cram session. This has been definitely established. What is more, a night a week for a month will return better dividends than crowding your study into a shorter period of time.
- Locate the place of the exam – You have been sent a notice telling you when and where to report for the examination. If the location is in a different town or otherwise unfamiliar to you, it would be well to inquire the best route and learn something about the building.
- Relax the night before the test – Allow your mind to rest. Do not study at all that night. Plan some mild recreation or diversion; then go to bed early and get a good night's sleep.
- Get up early enough to make a leisurely trip to the place for the test – This way unforeseen events, traffic snarls, unfamiliar buildings, etc. will not upset you.
- Dress comfortably – A written test is not a fashion show. You will be known by number and not by name, so wear something comfortable.
- Leave excess paraphernalia at home – Shopping bags and odd bundles will get in your way. You need bring only the items mentioned in the official notice you received; usually everything you need is provided. Do not bring reference books to the exam. They will only confuse those last minutes and be taken away from you when in the test room.
- Arrive somewhat ahead of time – If because of transportation schedules you must get there very early, bring a newspaper or magazine to take your mind off yourself while waiting.
- Locate the examination room – When you have found the proper room, you will be directed to the seat or part of the room where you will sit. Sometimes you are given a sheet of instructions to read while you are waiting. Do not fill out any forms until you are told to do so; just read them and be prepared.
- Relax and prepare to listen to the instructions
- If you have any physical problem that may keep you from doing your best, be sure to tell the test administrator. If you are sick or in poor health, you really cannot do your best on the exam. You can come back and take the test some other time.

VII. AT THE TEST

The day of the test is here and you have the test booklet in your hand. The temptation to get going is very strong. Caution! There is more to success than knowing the right answers. You must know how to identify your papers and understand variations in the type of short-answer question used in this particular examination. Follow these suggestions for maximum results from your efforts:

1) Cooperate with the monitor

The test administrator has a duty to create a situation in which you can be as much at ease as possible. He will give instructions, tell you when to begin, check to see that you are marking your answer sheet correctly, and so on. He is not there to guard you, although he will see that your competitors do not take unfair advantage. He wants to help you do your best.

2) Listen to all instructions

Don't jump the gun! Wait until you understand all directions. In most civil service tests you get more time than you need to answer the questions. So don't be in a hurry. Read each word of instructions until you clearly understand the meaning. Study the examples, listen to all announcements and follow directions. Ask questions if you do not understand what to do.

3) Identify your papers

Civil service exams are usually identified by number only. You will be assigned a number; you must not put your name on your test papers. Be sure to copy your number correctly. Since more than one exam may be given, copy your exact examination title.

4) Plan your time

Unless you are told that a test is a "speed" or "rate of work" test, speed itself is usually not important. Time enough to answer all the questions will be provided, but this does not mean that you have all day. An overall time limit has been set. Divide the total time (in minutes) by the number of questions to determine the approximate time you have for each question.

5) Do not linger over difficult questions

If you come across a difficult question, mark it with a paper clip (useful to have along) and come back to it when you have been through the booklet. One caution if you do this – be sure to skip a number on your answer sheet as well. Check often to be sure that you have not lost your place and that you are marking in the row numbered the same as the question you are answering.

6) Read the questions

Be sure you know what the question asks! Many capable people are unsuccessful because they failed to *read* the questions correctly.

7) Answer all questions

Unless you have been instructed that a penalty will be deducted for incorrect answers, it is better to guess than to omit a question.

8) Speed tests

It is often better NOT to guess on speed tests. It has been found that on timed tests people are tempted to spend the last few seconds before time is called in marking answers at random – without even reading them – in the hope of picking up a few extra points. To discourage this practice, the instructions may warn you that your score will be "corrected" for guessing. That is, a penalty will be applied. The incorrect answers will be deducted from the correct ones, or some other penalty formula will be used.

9) Review your answers

If you finish before time is called, go back to the questions you guessed or omitted to give them further thought. Review other answers if you have time.

10) Return your test materials

If you are ready to leave before others have finished or time is called, take ALL your materials to the monitor and leave quietly. Never take any test material with you. The monitor can discover whose papers are not complete, and taking a test booklet may be grounds for disqualification.

VIII. EXAMINATION TECHNIQUES

1) Read the general instructions carefully. These are usually printed on the first page of the exam booklet. As a rule, these instructions refer to the timing of the examination; the fact that you should not start work until the signal and must stop work at a signal, etc. If there are any *special* instructions, such as a choice of questions to be answered, make sure that you note this instruction carefully.

2) When you are ready to start work on the examination, that is as soon as the signal has been given, read the instructions to each question booklet, underline any key words or phrases, such as *least*, *best*, *outline*, *describe* and the like. In this way you will tend to answer as requested rather than discover on reviewing your paper that you *listed without describing*, that you selected the *worst* choice rather than the *best* choice, etc.

3) If the examination is of the objective or multiple-choice type – that is, each question will also give a series of possible answers: A, B, C or D, and you are called upon to select the best answer and write the letter next to that answer on your answer paper – it is advisable to start answering each question in turn. There may be anywhere from 50 to 100 such questions in the three or four hours allotted and you can see how much time would be taken if you read through all the questions before beginning to answer any. Furthermore, if you come across a question or group of questions which you know would be difficult to answer, it would undoubtedly affect your handling of all the other questions.

4) If the examination is of the essay type and contains but a few questions, it is a moot point as to whether you should read all the questions before starting to answer any one. Of course, if you are given a choice – say five out of seven and the like – then it is essential to read all the questions so you can eliminate the two that are most difficult. If, however, you are asked to answer all the questions, there may be danger in trying to answer the easiest one first because you may find that you will spend too much time on it. The best technique is to answer the first question, then proceed to the second, etc.

5) Time your answers. Before the exam begins, write down the time it started, then add the time allowed for the examination and write down the time it must be completed, then divide the time available somewhat as follows:

- If 3-1/2 hours are allowed, that would be 210 minutes. If you have 80 objective-type questions, that would be an average of 2-1/2 minutes per question. Allow yourself no more than 2 minutes per question, or a total of 160 minutes, which will permit about 50 minutes to review.
- If for the time allotment of 210 minutes there are 7 essay questions to answer, that would average about 30 minutes a question. Give yourself only 25 minutes per question so that you have about 35 minutes to review.

6) The most important instruction is to *read each question* and make sure you know what is wanted. The second most important instruction is to *time yourself properly* so that you answer every question. The third most important instruction is to *answer every question.* Guess if you have to but include something for each question. Remember that you will receive no credit for a blank and will probably receive some credit if you write something in answer to an essay question. If you guess a letter – say "B" for a multiple-choice question – you may have guessed right. If you leave a blank as an answer to a multiple-choice question, the examiners may respect your feelings but it will not add a point to your score. Some exams may penalize you for wrong answers, so in such cases *only*, you may not want to guess unless you have some basis for your answer.

7) Suggestions
   a. Objective-type questions
      1. Examine the question booklet for proper sequence of pages and questions
      2. Read all instructions carefully
      3. Skip any question which seems too difficult; return to it after all other questions have been answered
      4. Apportion your time properly; do not spend too much time on any single question or group of questions
      5. Note and underline key words – *all, most, fewest, least, best, worst, same, opposite,* etc.
      6. Pay particular attention to negatives
      7. Note unusual option, e.g., unduly long, short, complex, different or similar in content to the body of the question
      8. Observe the use of "hedging" words – *probably, may, most likely,* etc.
      9. Make sure that your answer is put next to the same number as the question
      10. Do not second-guess unless you have good reason to believe the second answer is definitely more correct
      11. Cross out original answer if you decide another answer is more accurate; do not erase until you are ready to hand your paper in
      12. Answer all questions; guess unless instructed otherwise
      13. Leave time for review

   b. Essay questions
      1. Read each question carefully
      2. Determine exactly what is wanted. Underline key words or phrases.
      3. Decide on outline or paragraph answer

4. Include many different points and elements unless asked to develop any one or two points or elements
5. Show impartiality by giving pros and cons unless directed to select one side only
6. Make and write down any assumptions you find necessary to answer the questions
7. Watch your English, grammar, punctuation and choice of words
8. Time your answers; don't crowd material

8) Answering the essay question

Most essay questions can be answered by framing the specific response around several key words or ideas. Here are a few such key words or ideas:

M's: manpower, materials, methods, money, management
P's: purpose, program, policy, plan, procedure, practice, problems, pitfalls, personnel, public relations

a. Six basic steps in handling problems:
    1. Preliminary plan and background development
    2. Collect information, data and facts
    3. Analyze and interpret information, data and facts
    4. Analyze and develop solutions as well as make recommendations
    5. Prepare report and sell recommendations
    6. Install recommendations and follow up effectiveness

b. Pitfalls to avoid
    1. *Taking things for granted* – A statement of the situation does not necessarily imply that each of the elements is necessarily true; for example, a complaint may be invalid and biased so that all that can be taken for granted is that a complaint has been registered
    2. *Considering only one side of a situation* – Wherever possible, indicate several alternatives and then point out the reasons you selected the best one
    3. *Failing to indicate follow up* – Whenever your answer indicates action on your part, make certain that you will take proper follow-up action to see how successful your recommendations, procedures or actions turn out to be
    4. *Taking too long in answering any single question* – Remember to time your answers properly

IX. AFTER THE TEST

Scoring procedures differ in detail among civil service jurisdictions although the general principles are the same. Whether the papers are hand-scored or graded by machine we have described, they are nearly always graded by number. That is, the person who marks the paper knows only the number – never the name – of the applicant. Not until all the papers have been graded will they be matched with names. If other tests, such as training and experience or oral interview ratings have been given, scores will be combined. Different parts of the examination usually have different weights. For example, the written test might count 60 percent of the final grade, and a rating of training and experience 40 percent. In many jurisdictions, veterans will have a certain number of points added to their grades.

After the final grade has been determined, the names are placed in grade order and an eligible list is established. There are various methods for resolving ties between those who get the same final grade – probably the most common is to place first the name of the person whose application was received first. Job offers are made from the eligible list in the order the names appear on it. You will be notified of your grade and your rank as soon as all these computations have been made. This will be done as rapidly as possible.

People who are found to meet the requirements in the announcement are called "eligibles." Their names are put on a list of eligible candidates. An eligible's chances of getting a job depend on how high he stands on this list and how fast agencies are filling jobs from the list.

When a job is to be filled from a list of eligibles, the agency asks for the names of people on the list of eligibles for that job. When the civil service commission receives this request, it sends to the agency the names of the three people highest on this list. Or, if the job to be filled has specialized requirements, the office sends the agency the names of the top three persons who meet these requirements from the general list.

The appointing officer makes a choice from among the three people whose names were sent to him. If the selected person accepts the appointment, the names of the others are put back on the list to be considered for future openings.

That is the rule in hiring from all kinds of eligible lists, whether they are for typist, carpenter, chemist, or something else. For every vacancy, the appointing officer has his choice of any one of the top three eligibles on the list. This explains why the person whose name is on top of the list sometimes does not get an appointment when some of the persons lower on the list do. If the appointing officer chooses the second or third eligible, the No. 1 eligible does not get a job at once, but stays on the list until he is appointed or the list is terminated.

X. HOW TO PASS THE INTERVIEW TEST

The examination for which you applied requires an oral interview test. You have already taken the written test and you are now being called for the interview test – the final part of the formal examination.

You may think that it is not possible to prepare for an interview test and that there are no procedures to follow during an interview. Our purpose is to point out some things you can do in advance that will help you and some good rules to follow and pitfalls to avoid while you are being interviewed.

What is an interview supposed to test?

The written examination is designed to test the technical knowledge and competence of the candidate; the oral is designed to evaluate intangible qualities, not readily measured otherwise, and to establish a list showing the relative fitness of each candidate – as measured against his competitors – for the position sought. Scoring is not on the basis of "right" and "wrong," but on a sliding scale of values ranging from "not passable" to "outstanding." As a matter of fact, it is possible to achieve a relatively low score without a single "incorrect" answer because of evident weakness in the qualities being measured.

Occasionally, an examination may consist entirely of an oral test – either an individual or a group oral. In such cases, information is sought concerning the technical knowledges and abilities of the candidate, since there has been no written examination for this purpose. More commonly, however, an oral test is used to supplement a written examination.

Who conducts interviews?

The composition of oral boards varies among different jurisdictions. In nearly all, a representative of the personnel department serves as chairman. One of the members of the board may be a representative of the department in which the candidate would work. In some cases, "outside experts" are used, and, frequently, a businessman or some other representative of the general public is asked to serve. Labor and management or other special groups may be represented. The aim is to secure the services of experts in the appropriate field.

However the board is composed, it is a good idea (and not at all improper or unethical) to ascertain in advance of the interview who the members are and what groups they represent. When you are introduced to them, you will have some idea of their backgrounds and interests, and at least you will not stutter and stammer over their names.

What should be done before the interview?

While knowledge about the board members is useful and takes some of the surprise element out of the interview, there is other preparation which is more substantive. It *is* possible to prepare for an oral interview – in several ways:

1) Keep a copy of your application and review it carefully before the interview

This may be the only document before the oral board, and the starting point of the interview. Know what education and experience you have listed there, and the sequence and dates of all of it. Sometimes the board will ask you to review the highlights of your experience for them; you should not have to hem and haw doing it.

2) Study the class specification and the examination announcement

Usually, the oral board has one or both of these to guide them. The qualities, characteristics or knowledges required by the position sought are stated in these documents. They offer valuable clues as to the nature of the oral interview. For example, if the job involves supervisory responsibilities, the announcement will usually indicate that knowledge of modern supervisory methods and the qualifications of the candidate as a supervisor will be tested. If so, you can expect such questions, frequently in the form of a hypothetical situation which you are expected to solve. NEVER go into an oral without knowledge of the duties and responsibilities of the job you seek.

3) Think through each qualification required

Try to visualize the kind of questions you would ask if you were a board member. How well could you answer them? Try especially to appraise your own knowledge and background in each area, *measured against the job sought*, and identify any areas in which you are weak. Be critical and realistic – do not flatter yourself.

4) Do some general reading in areas in which you feel you may be weak

For example, if the job involves supervision and your past experience has NOT, some general reading in supervisory methods and practices, particularly in the field of human relations, might be useful. Do NOT study agency procedures or detailed manuals. The oral board will be testing your understanding and capacity, not your memory.

5) Get a good night's sleep and watch your general health and mental attitude

You will want a clear head at the interview. Take care of a cold or any other minor ailment, and of course, no hangovers.

What should be done on the day of the interview?

Now comes the day of the interview itself. Give yourself plenty of time to get there. Plan to arrive somewhat ahead of the scheduled time, particularly if your appointment is in the fore part of the day. If a previous candidate fails to appear, the board might be ready for you a bit early. By early afternoon an oral board is almost invariably behind schedule if there are many candidates, and you may have to wait. Take along a book or magazine to read, or your application to review, but leave any extraneous material in the waiting room when you go in for your interview. In any event, relax and compose yourself.

The matter of dress is important. The board is forming impressions about you – from your experience, your manners, your attitude, and your appearance. Give your personal appearance careful attention. Dress your best, but not your flashiest. Choose conservative, appropriate clothing, and be sure it is immaculate. This is a business interview, and your appearance should indicate that you regard it as such. Besides, being well groomed and properly dressed will help boost your confidence.

Sooner or later, someone will call your name and escort you into the interview room. *This is it.* From here on you are on your own. It is too late for any more preparation. But remember, you asked for this opportunity to prove your fitness, and you are here because your request was granted.

What happens when you go in?

The usual sequence of events will be as follows: The clerk (who is often the board stenographer) will introduce you to the chairman of the oral board, who will introduce you to the other members of the board. Acknowledge the introductions before you sit down. Do not be surprised if you find a microphone facing you or a stenotypist sitting by. Oral interviews are usually recorded in the event of an appeal or other review.

Usually the chairman of the board will open the interview by reviewing the highlights of your education and work experience from your application – primarily for the benefit of the other members of the board, as well as to get the material into the record. Do not interrupt or comment unless there is an error or significant misinterpretation; if that is the case, do not hesitate. But do not quibble about insignificant matters. Also, he will usually ask you some question about your education, experience or your present job – partly to get you to start talking and to establish the interviewing "rapport." He may start the actual questioning, or turn it over to one of the other members. Frequently, each member undertakes the questioning on a particular area, one in which he is perhaps most competent, so you can expect each member to participate in the examination. Because time is limited, you may also expect some rather abrupt switches in the direction the questioning takes, so do not be upset by it. Normally, a board member will not pursue a single line of questioning unless he discovers a particular strength or weakness.

After each member has participated, the chairman will usually ask whether any member has any further questions, then will ask you if you have anything you wish to add. Unless you are expecting this question, it may floor you. Worse, it may start you off on an extended, extemporaneous speech. The board is not usually seeking more information. The question is principally to offer you a last opportunity to present further qualifications or to indicate that you have nothing to add. So, if you feel that a significant qualification or characteristic has been overlooked, it is proper to point it out in a sentence or so. Do not compliment the board on the thoroughness of their examination – they have been sketchy, and you know it. If you wish, merely say, "No thank you, I have nothing further to add." This is a point where you can "talk yourself out" of a good impression or fail to present an important bit of information. Remember, *you close the interview yourself.*

The chairman will then say, "That is all, Mr. _______, thank you." Do not be startled; the interview is over, and quicker than you think. Thank him, gather your belongings and take your leave. Save your sigh of relief for the other side of the door.

How to put your best foot forward

Throughout this entire process, you may feel that the board individually and collectively is trying to pierce your defenses, seek out your hidden weaknesses and embarrass and confuse you. Actually, this is not true. They are obliged to make an appraisal of your qualifications for the job you are seeking, and they want to see you in your best light. Remember, they must interview all candidates and a non-cooperative candidate may become a failure in spite of their best efforts to bring out his qualifications. Here are 15 suggestions that will help you:

1) Be natural – Keep your attitude confident, not cocky

If you are not confident that you can do the job, do not expect the board to be. Do not apologize for your weaknesses, try to bring out your strong points. The board is interested in a positive, not negative, presentation. Cockiness will antagonize any board member and make him wonder if you are covering up a weakness by a false show of strength.

2) Get comfortable, but don't lounge or sprawl

Sit erectly but not stiffly. A careless posture may lead the board to conclude that you are careless in other things, or at least that you are not impressed by the importance of the occasion. Either conclusion is natural, even if incorrect. Do not fuss with your clothing, a pencil or an ashtray. Your hands may occasionally be useful to emphasize a point; do not let them become a point of distraction.

3) Do not wisecrack or make small talk

This is a serious situation, and your attitude should show that you consider it as such. Further, the time of the board is limited – they do not want to waste it, and neither should you.

4) Do not exaggerate your experience or abilities

In the first place, from information in the application or other interviews and sources, the board may know more about you than you think. Secondly, you probably will not get away with it. An experienced board is rather adept at spotting such a situation, so do not take the chance.

5) If you know a board member, do not make a point of it, yet do not hide it

Certainly you are not fooling him, and probably not the other members of the board. Do not try to take advantage of your acquaintanceship – it will probably do you little good.

6) Do not dominate the interview

Let the board do that. They will give you the clues – do not assume that you have to do all the talking. Realize that the board has a number of questions to ask you, and do not try to take up all the interview time by showing off your extensive knowledge of the answer to the first one.

7) Be attentive

You only have 20 minutes or so, and you should keep your attention at its sharpest throughout. When a member is addressing a problem or question to you, give him your undivided attention. Address your reply principally to him, but do not exclude the other board members.

8) Do not interrupt

A board member may be stating a problem for you to analyze. He will ask you a question when the time comes. Let him state the problem, and wait for the question.

9) Make sure you understand the question

Do not try to answer until you are sure what the question is. If it is not clear, restate it in your own words or ask the board member to clarify it for you. However, do not haggle about minor elements.

10) Reply promptly but not hastily

A common entry on oral board rating sheets is “candidate responded readily,” or “candidate hesitated in replies.” Respond as promptly and quickly as you can, but do not jump to a hasty, ill-considered answer.

11) Do not be peremptory in your answers

A brief answer is proper – but do not fire your answer back. That is a losing game from your point of view. The board member can probably ask questions much faster than you can answer them.

12) Do not try to create the answer you think the board member wants

He is interested in what kind of mind you have and how it works – not in playing games. Furthermore, he can usually spot this practice and will actually grade you down on it.

13) Do not switch sides in your reply merely to agree with a board member

Frequently, a member will take a contrary position merely to draw you out and to see if you are willing and able to defend your point of view. Do not start a debate, yet do not surrender a good position. If a position is worth taking, it is worth defending.

14) Do not be afraid to admit an error in judgment if you are shown to be wrong

The board knows that you are forced to reply without any opportunity for careful consideration. Your answer may be demonstrably wrong. If so, admit it and get on with the interview.

15) Do not dwell at length on your present job

The opening question may relate to your present assignment. Answer the question but do not go into an extended discussion. You are being examined for a *new* job, not your present one. As a matter of fact, try to phrase ALL your answers in terms of the job for which you are being examined.

Basis of Rating

Probably you will forget most of these "do's" and "don'ts" when you walk into the oral interview room. Even remembering them all will not ensure you a passing grade. Perhaps you did not have the qualifications in the first place. But remembering them will help you to put your best foot forward, without treading on the toes of the board members.

Rumor and popular opinion to the contrary notwithstanding, an oral board wants you to make the best appearance possible. They know you are under pressure – but they also want to see how you respond to it as a guide to what your reaction would be under the pressures of the job you seek. They will be influenced by the degree of poise you display, the personal traits you show and the manner in which you respond.

ABOUT THIS BOOK

This book contains tests divided into Examination Sections. Go through each test, answering every question in the margin. At the end of each test look at the answer key and check your answers. On the ones you got wrong, look at the right answer choice and learn. Do not fill in the answers first. Do not memorize the questions and answers, but understand the answer and principles involved. On your test, the questions will likely be different from the samples. Questions are changed and new ones added. If you understand these past questions you should have success with any changes that arise. Tests may consist of several types of questions. We have additional books on each subject should more study be advisable or necessary for you. Finally, the more you study, the better prepared you will be. This book is intended to be the last thing you study before you walk into the examination room. Prior study of relevant texts is also recommended. NLC publishes some of these in our Fundamental Series. Knowledge and good sense are important factors in passing your exam. Good luck also helps. So now study this Passbook, absorb the material contained within and take that knowledge into the examination. Then do your best to pass that exam.

EXAMINATION SECTION

EXAMINATION SECTION
TEST 1

DIRECTIONS: Each question or incomplete statement is followed by several suggested answers or completions. Select the one that BEST answers the question or completes the statement. *PRINT THE LETTER OF THE CORRECT ANSWER IN THE SPACE AT THE RIGHT.*

1. C. trachomatis, a small bacterium which is the leading cause of epididymitis in men under age 35, is 1.____

   A. a gram-negative intracellular diplococcus
   B. not a sexually transmitted disease
   C. present in 80% of men with Reiter's syndrome
   D. always symptomatic

2. A male patient 32 years of age had urethral discharge and dysuria. The discharge was yellow and brown. The patient was treated with penicillin. A thin, clear discharge continued following penicillin treatment. 2.____
   This is MOST likely due to

   A. inadequate treatment
   B. concurrent infection by C. trachomatis
   C. recurrence of gonococcal urethritis
   D. urethral inflammation

3. A female patient, 23 years of age, comes into the office with complaints of dysuria, suprapubic pain, urgency and nocturia. 3.____
   The MOST common cause of her urinary tract infection (cystitis) is

   A. neisseria gonorrhea B. chlamydia trachomatis
   C. pseudomonas D. escherichia coli

4. Which one of the following drugs may be used in the case described in the previous question? 4.____

   A. Sulfonamides
   B. Trimethoprim-sulfamethoxazole
   C. Nitrofurantoin
   D. All of the above

5. A case of nephrotic syndrome usually presents with massive edena, hypoalbuminemia, hyperlipidemia, anemia, and heavy protein loss. 5.____
   Regarding protein loss in this condition, there is USUALLY a loss of _______ gram(s) of protein over 24 hours.

   A. 4-10 B. 1 C. 0.5 D. 1.2

6. A male patient, 57 years of age, comes in with complaints of hesitancy, urgency, dribbling of urine, loss of force and caliber of stream, and a feeling of incomplete emptying of the bladder. According to the patient, he has had a rapid onset and progression of symptoms. You suspect prostatic cancer. 6.____
   A useful marker of prostatic cancer.

   A. testosterone B. parathyroid hormone
   C. acid phosphatase D. alkaline phosphatase

Questions 7-9.

DIRECTIONS: Questions 7 through 9 are to be answered on the basis of the following information.

A female patient, 34 years of age, develops dysuria, urgency, and flank pain. Two days later, she starts having nausea and vomiting with fever and chills. Her urinary symptoms persist. She is brought in by her husband, who states that before this episode, his wife was fine.

7. You would suspect 7.____

A. chronic cystitis
B. acute pyelonephritis
C. renal calculi
D. urethritis

8. Proper treatment of this patient should include 8.____

A. hydration
B. control of pain and fever
C. urine for culture and sensitivity
D. all of the above

9. The treatment of choice for this patient would be 9.____

A. penicillin and tetracycline
B. erythromycin and chlorampherico!
C. ampicillin and an aminoglycoside
D. none of the above

10. The MOST common cause of anemia in the elderly is 10.____

A. iron deficiency
B. folate deficiency
C. anemia of chronic disease
D. pernicious anemia

11. In age-related postmenopausal osteoporosis, there is an increased incidence of vertebral fractures. 11.____
This is MAINLY due to

A. decreased calcium absorption
B. decreased parathyroid function
C. trabecular bone loss
D. all of the above

12. An 81-year-old patient has the following lab results: low serum iron, low total iron binding capacity, high ferritin level, hypochromic anemia. 12.____
The patient PROBABLY suffers from

A. anemia of chronic disease
B. sideroblastic anemia
C. pernicious anemia
D. iron deficiency

13. Elderly patients should be protected from influenza. The influenza vaccine should be received every 13.____

A. 5 months
B. year
C. 5 years
D. 2 years

14. An 87-year-old man is suffering from severe dementia. According to the nurse, he is not cooperative at all and is having persistent urinary incontinence. 14.____
This patient MOST likely suffers from ______ incontinence.

A. stress
B. functional
C. urge
D. overflow

15. Among the elderly population, conditions such as diabetic retinopathy, glaucoma, and cataracts are common and may result in blindness. 15.____
Which of the following tests should be performed ROUTINELY to screen for these conditions?

A. Test of visual acuity
B. Performing opthalmic examination
C. Checking intraocular pressure
D. All of the above

16. Alzheimer's disease involves 16.____

A. progressive worsening of memory and other cognitive functions
B. deficits in two or more areas of cognition
C. no disturbance of consciousness
D. all of the above

17. Parents bring their 17-year-old boy in because they suspect that he is on drugs. On questioning, he reveals that after taking a certain drug he feels *so good,* almost orgasmic, followed by euphoria and a feeling of mental alertness. 17.____
He is PROBABLY taking

A. naloxone
B. heroin
C. cocaine
D. marijuana

18. A child displays microcephaly, prenatal/postnatal growth deficiency, short palpebral fissures, cardiac defects, anomalies of the inner ear, and mental retardation. 18.____
The mother is an alcoholic.
The child PROBABLY suffers from

A. Down's syndrome
B. cretinism
C. fetal alcohol syndrome
D. protein deficiency

19. Cocaine abuse during pregnancy causes 19.____

A. low birth weight
B. increased incidence of SIDS
C. behavioral abnormalities
D. all of the above

20. A 27-year-old male comes in with pink, purple, and non-pigmented nodular skin lesions on his extremities, skin, and viscera associated with lymphatic obstruction. The patient suffers from AIDS. The MOST likely diagnosis is 20.____

A. atopic dermatitis
B. Kaposi's sarcoma
C. contact dermatitis
D. all of the above

21. A 24-year-old male comes to your office complaining of shortness of breath and a temperature of 40°C. He also gives a history of hemophilia and a positive HIV ELISA test a year ago. Which of the following should be included in the differential diagnosis? 21.____

A. Cytomegalovirus pneumonitis
B. Viral pneumonia
C. P. carinii pneumonia
D. All of the above

22. The goals of evaluating a patient with HIV should include 22.____

A. evaluation of immune system
B. identification of infections and their complications
C. institution of approved antiretroviral therapy
D. all of the above

23. Which of the following is MOST important in taking a thorough history of an HIV patient? 23.____

A. History of past immunizations
B. History of sexually transmitted diseases
C. Family history of HIV
D. Age at the time of first intercourse

24. A 28-year-old male comes to your office with a complaint of candidiasis of the esophagus, trachea, bronchi, and lungs. He was under treatment for these conditions with another doctor but showed no improvement. He suffers from AIDS. The BEST treatment for candidiasis in this patient would be 24.____

A. nystatin
B. clotrimazole
C. ketoconazole
D. all of the above

25. You are treating a 45-year-old male who is HIV positive with symptoms of dizziness, weakness, headaches, and fever. You suspect toxoplasma encephalitis. Drugs that are useful in treatment include 25.____

A. sulfadiazine
B. amphotericin B
C. 5-flucytosine
D. none of the above

KEY (CORRECT ANSWERS)

1. C
2. B
3. D
4. D
5. A
6. C
7. B
8. D
9. C
10. A
11. D
12. A
13. B
14. B
15. D
16. D
17. C
18. C
19. D
20. B
21. D
22. D
23. B
24. D
25. A

TEST 2

DIRECTIONS: Each question or incomplete statement is followed by several suggested answers or completions. Select the one that BEST answers the question or completes the statement. *PRINT THE LETTER OF THE CORRECT ANSWER IN THE SPACE AT THE RIGHT.*

1. A 23-year-old patient with the clinical manifestations of lymph node disease with lung and bone marrow involvement is diagnosed with tuberculosis. 1.____
   Which one of the following is the BEST drug for management of tuberculosis?

   A. Streptomycin
   B. Isoniazid and rifampicin
   C. Ethambutor and pyrazinamide
   D. All of the above

2. Disseminated manifestations often caused by secondary syphilis are COMMONLY seen in the 2.____

   A. skin
   B. mouth
   C. genitalia
   D. all of the above

3. Breast cancer is one of the most common cancers in women. 3.____
   The clinical presentation of breast cancer involves

   A. a painless lump
   B. nipple discharge
   C. nipple retraction
   D. all of the above

4. HIV infection may be transmitted by 4.____

   A. feces
   B. semen
   C. casual contact
   D. all of the above

5. Which one of the following studies is diagnostic to rule out intracranial lesions? 5.____

   A. Brain biopsy
   B. Lumbar puncture
   C. Pneumoencephalogram
   D. Computorial tomography of the brain

6. A 23-year-old patient comes in with neurologic signs and symptoms. A CT scan of the brain reveals no intracranial lesions. 6.____
   The NEXT test that should be done on this patient is a

   A. brain biopsy
   B. lumbar puncture
   C. pneumoencephalogram
   D. none of the above

7. The MOST common complication occurring after an appendectomy is 7.____

   A. paralytic ileus
   B. retained appendix or foreign body
   C. wound infection
   D. none of the above

8. In cases of mechanical bowel obstruction, ______ would be evident by looking at a radiograph. 8.____

   A. dilated small intestine with gas scattered throughout
   B. localized air fluid levels
   C. dilated large intestine with air scattered throughout
   D. all of the above

9. Benefits of the cessation of smoking before an operation include that 9.____

   A. it decreases blood levels of carbon monoxide
   B. it leaves more hemoglobin available for oxygen transport
   C. the paralyzing effect of smoke on mucociliary transport may be improved
   D. all of the above

10. Fresh frozen plasma or vitamin K is given to REVERSE the effects of 10.____

    A. coumadin
    B. protamine
    C. heparin
    D. none of the above

11. When considering organ donation for heart/lung transplants, it is IMPORTANT that the donor 11.____

    A. be free from active infections
    B. and recipient be of compatible weight and body build
    C. have no previous history of communicable disease
    D. all of the above

12. An 18-year-old male student sustained a blow to the head during a fight and become unconscious. On the way to the hospital, he woke up with no neurologic deficits. He then had a gradual deterioration of consciousness that progressed to coma and death. This is compatible with the diagnosis of 12.____

    A. epidural hematoma
    B. skull fracture
    C. subdural hematoma
    D. spinal cord injury

13. What would you recommend to a 54 year-old lady with herniation of a lumbar disc? 13.____

    A. Exercise
    B. Physical therapy
    C. Bedrest
    D. Calcium supplements

14. An 83-year-old patient comes to the office with the complaint of dull, aching, constant, left lower quadrant pain. The MOST likely diagnosis is 14.____

    A. volvulus
    B. diverticulitis
    C. urinary tract infection
    D. colon cancer

15. The MOST common complication of acute pancreatitis is 15.____

    A. abscess
    B. pseudocyst
    C. cellulitis
    D. all of the above

16. ______ increase(s) the anticoagulant effect of warfarin (coumadin) by inhibition of clotting factors and platelet adhesiveness. 16.____

A. Barbiturates
B. Cholestyramine
C. Vitamin K (large doses)
D. Salicylates

17. Which of the following work by inhibition of cell wall synthesis to produce their antibacterial action? 17.____

I. Penicillin
II. Cephalosporin
III. Vitamin K

The CORRECT answer is:

A. I *only*
B. II *only*
C. I, II
D. I, III

18. The antibiotic tetracycline is 18.____

A. bacteriostatic
B. bactericidal
C. bacteriogenic
D. all of the above

19. Cimetidine, which is used in the treatment of gastric and duodenal ulcers and in hypersecretory states such as Zolinger Ellison syndrome can be given 19.____

A. parenterally
B. orally
C. rectally
D. all of the above

20. A 17-year-old boy is asthmatic and takes terbutaline for his attacks. 20.____
Which one of the following drugs can be given to him prophylactically to prevent attacks and NOT for acute management?

A. Epinephrine
B. Theophylline
C. Cromolyn sodium
D. Terbutaline

21. A 23-year-old female comes to you. She suffers from genital herpes. 21.____
The MOST effective drug in the treatment of herpes is

A. acyclovir
B. amantadine
C. 5-fluorouracil
D. rimantadin

22. A mother brings her 3-year-old boy to the clinic because she is worried about the boy's dental abnormality. According to her, the boy received an antibiotic for a long time. 22.____
The drug that would MOST likely cause a dental abnormality is

A. penicillin
B. tetracycline
C. erythromycin
D. streptomycin

23. Beta blockers can be used clinically to treat hypertension, angina, arrhythmias, and anxiety states. Beta blockers DECREASE 23.____

A. heart rate
B. myocardial contractility
C. cardiac output
D. all of the above

24. Beta blockers are CONTRAINDICATED in states of 24.____

A. hyperthyroidism
B. congestive heart failure
C. glaucoma
D. migraine headaches

25. Potassium sparing diuretics include 25.____

A. triamtere
B. spironolactone
C. amiloride HCl
D. all of the above

KEY (CORRECT ANSWERS)

1. D
2. D
3. D
4. B
5. D
6. B
7. C
8. B
9. D
10. A
11. D
12. A
13. C
14. B
15. B
16. D
17. C
18. A
19. B
20. C
21. A
22. B
23. D
24. B
25. D

EXAMINATION SECTION
TEST 1

DIRECTIONS: Each question or incomplete statement is followed by several suggested answers or completions. Select the one that BEST answers the question or completes the statement. *PRINT THE LETTER OF THE CORRECT ANSWER IN THE SPACE AT THE RIGHT.*

1. All of the following statements are true regarding vasodilator therapy with hydralazine and minoxidil in the treatment of hypertension EXCEPT: 1.____

   A. Impotence is a common side effect
   B. Orthostatic hypotension is not a common problem
   C. Decreased peripheral vascular resistance may occur
   D. Sympathetic reflexes reduce in effectiveness

2. A 32-year-old female suffers from severe hypertension. The MOST effective diuretic therapy you can advise for her is ______ diuretics. 2.____

   A. thiazide-like
   B. potassium sparing
   C. thiazide
   D. loop

3. Digitalis, when given to a patient with heart failure, would REDUCE 3.____

   A. cardiac output
   B. blood volume
   C. stroke volume
   D. all of the above

4. Digitalis, when given to a patient for a long time, tends to produce side effects, such as toxicity, that are potentially lethal. 4.____
   Such side effects

   A. are greater with advanced heart disease
   B. are exacerbated by hyperkalemia
   C. occur in 20% of patients digitalized
   D. all of the above

5. A 42-year-old male comes to the office with complaints of postural hypotension, muscle cramps, vascular headaches, and esophageal spasms. A few weeks ago, he started exercising due to chest pain to keep himself healthy, and is at the moment taking nitroglycerine for chest pain and an NSAID. 5.____
   The MOST likely reason for these symptoms is

   A. overexercise
   B. adverse reaction due to nitroglycerine
   C. reaction due to NSAID
   D. all of the above

6. Nitroglycerine may be taken 6.____

   A. topically
   B. sublingually
   C. orally
   D. all of the above

7. Indications for the use of calcium channel blockers include 7.____
   I. cardiac arrhythmias
   II. hypertension
   III. angina
   The CORRECT answer is:

8. Which of the following drugs is used in the termination of an acute attack of gout? 8.____
   A. Aspirin
   B. Colchicine
   C. Acetaminophen
   D. Verapamil

9. All of the following statements are true regarding bretylium in the treatment of ventricular arrhythmias EXCEPT: 9.____
   A. Available for parenteral use only
   B. Use should not exceed 5 days
   C. First line antiarrhythmatic
   D. Use in conditions that are unresponsive to lidocaine and procainamide

10. Quinidine may NOT be used in cases of congestive heart failure and myasthenia gravis because it has a _______ ionotropic effect and _______ cardiac action. 10.____
    A. positive; depresses
    B. positive; stimulates
    C. negative; depresses
    D. negative; stimulates

11. ALL women are considered to be at high risk for breast cancer and should begin a schedule of annual mammography at age 11.____
    A. 20
    B. 40
    C. 50
    D. 30

12. A 16-year-old boy experienced excruciating pain in the testicular region while playing baseball. It was diagnosed to be testicular torsion. 12.____
    Which of the following statements is TRUE regarding this diagnosis?
    A. Patients of testicular torsion exhibit a tender testicle in transverse position
    B. The affected testicle is lower in the scrotum than the unaffected one
    C. Pain is relieved by scrotal elevation
    D. All of the above

13. Regarding patients about to undergo surgery who are well-controlled for seizures on anticonvulsant therapy, 13.____
    A. the anticonvulsant therapy should be continued via parenteral route until patient is tolerating oral feedings
    B. the patient may have surgery without being evaluated by a neurologist for clearance
    C. Uremia, hyponatremia, and hypernatremia have to be carefully managed because they predispose to seizures
    D. All of the above

14. Blood glucose level is the major determinant for the insulin requirement of a diabetic patient undergoing surgery. 14.____
    The level at which additional insulin may be given should be _______ mg/dl
    A. 250
    B. 350
    C. 150
    D. 100

15. A 22-year-old man is bitten by a cat. He reports that the last time he was immunized against tetanus was 10 years ago. 15.____
The treatment of this patient should include

A. IM administration of 0.5 ml tetanus toxoid
B. IM administration of 250 units of tetanus immuno-globulin
C. careful debridement and copious irrigation of wound
D. all of the above

16. Possible problems with inadequate wound drainage include 16.____

A. bacterial growth
B. loss of vascularity
C. tissue necrosis
D. all of the above

17. Which of the following is an indication for surgery in patients with duodenal ulcers? 17.____

A. Severe, persistent or recurrent bleeding
B. Gastric output obstruction
C. Perforation of duodenal wall
D. All of the above

18. Common causes of intestinal obstruction in adults include 18.____

A. adhesions and hernias
B. volvulus
C. intersusception
D. none of the above

19. Which of the following conditions would indicate traumatic injury to the ureter, kidneys, or bladder? 19.____

A. Gross hematuria on inspection of urine
B. White blood cells on microscopic examination
C. Increased urine specific gravity
D. Increased bacteria on microscopic examination

20. Thorax tumors can often be easily resected if 20.____
I. they are located towards the periphery
II. they are malignant
III. there is involvement of hilar nodes only
The CORRECT answer is:

A. I *only*
B. I, II
C. I, III
D. II, III

21. DSM-IIIR is a WIDELY used system for 21.____

A. distinguishing sanity from insanity
B. classifying psychiatric disorders
C. identifying causes of abnormal behavior
D. all of the above

22. The basic defense mechanism identified by Freud in which motives and feelings unacceptable to the self are unconsciously attributed to others instead is called 22.____

A. denial
B. rejection
C. displacement
D. projection

23. Forcing thoughts, memories, and feelings into the unconscious and keeping them out of awareness is referred to as 23.____

A. regression
B. rationalization
C. repression
D. reaction formation

24. A form of denial in which we detach ourselves from our problems by analyzing them to an extreme, almost as if they concerned other people and did not bother us emotionally, is called 24.____

A. displacement
B. intellectualization
C. denial
D. rejection

25. Individuals who remain on guard towards others, are overconcerned with power and rank, feel that their view of the world is the correct one, and show mistrust of others are BASICALLY 25.____

A. paranoid
B. narcissistic
C. schizophrenic
D. borderline

KEY (CORRECT ANSWERS)

1. A
2. D
3. B
4. D
5. B
6. D
7. A
8. B
9. C
10. C
11. C
12. A
13. D
14. A
15. D
16. D
17. D
18. A
19. A
20. C
21. B
22. D
23. C
24. B
25. A

TEST 2

DIRECTIONS: Each question or incomplete statement is followed by several suggested answers or completions. Select the one that BEST answers the question or completes the statement. *PRINT THE LETTER OF THE CORRECT ANSWER IN THE SPACE AT THE RIGHT.*

1. In the four phase cycle, which represents the continuum of physiological arousal during sexual stimulation with regard to research by Masters and Johnson, the typical order is 1._____

   A. excitement, plateau, orgasm, resolution
   B. excitement, plateau, resolution, orgasm
   C. excitement, orgasm, plateau, resolution
   D. arousal, orgasm, refraction, resolution

2. A state of general sexual dysfunction in which there is an inability in women to derive erotic pleasure from sexual stimulation is called 2._____

   A. transvestism B. frigidity
   C. vaginismus D. sadomasochism

3. Which of the following is NOT a symptom of depression? 3._____

   A. Amnesia B. Feeling of worthlessness
   C. Loss of energy D. Sense of guilt

4. Stephanie, a nurse in the emergency department of a local hospital, complains that she feels apprehensive and fearful most of the time, but does not know why. She feels palpitations and breaks out in a sweat. 4._____
   She MOST likely suffers from

   A. somato form disorder B. dissociative disorder
   C. generalized anxiety D. phobic disorder

5. Mary believes that she will never again be able to do things she once enjoyed. She is apathetic, feels no appetite, and reports being tired all the time. She sits around doing nothing all day. 5._____
   She PROBABLY suffers from

   A. schizoid disorder
   B. manic depressive disorder
   C. depression
   D. conversion disorder

6. The presence of grandiose, jealous or persecutory delusions or hallucinations, for example, a feeling of being the king or owner of the world, MOST likely indicates _______ schizophrenia. 6._____

   A. catatonic B. disorganized
   C. paranoid D. undifferentiated

7. Hallucinations are perceptions believed to be real, despite evidence to the contrary. The MOST common type of hallucinations involve 7._____

   A. seeing visions B. hearing voices
   C. smelling odors D. bodily sensations

8. Somatoform disorders are characterized by physical symptoms that cannot be accounted for by any demonstrable physical evidence.
Examples of this disorder include 8.____

A. conversion disorder
B. psychogenic pain disorder
C. hypochondriasis
D. all of the above

9. *Mania* refers to a type of disorder characterized by 9.____

A. euphoria
B. hyperactivity
C. inflated self-esteem
D. all of the above

10. All of the following statements characterize post-traumatic stress disorder and adjustment disorder with anxious mood EXCEPT:
These disorders 10.____

A. can be seen in veterans
B. may be accompanied by impairment of social functioning
C. may persist long after the stress has abated
D. must be accompanied by depression

11. Management of a hospitalized patient who becomes hostile whenever his feelings about his illness are questioned or attempts to get to know him are made might include 11.____

A. telling the patient that his hostility is interfering with the physician-patient relationship
B. telling the patient that his anger is due to anxiety
C. allowing the patient to determine the degree of interpersonal distance
D. getting angry yourself

12. A 30-year-old man complains of panic attacks and anticipatory anxiety.
Which of the following drugs would provide effective treatment? 12.____

A. Haloperidol
B. Diazepam
C. Meprobamate
D. All of the above

13. All of the following are commonly observed features of schizophrenia EXCEPT 13.____

A. decreased appetite
B. thought blocking
C. delusions of influence
D. auditory hallucinations

14. A 22-year-old college student gets good grades but displays florid psychosis following the news of the death of his mother.
The MOST likely course for this patient's illness would be 14.____

A. chronic psychosis
B. chronic psychosis with remission and relapses
C. remission with return of good level of functioning
D. none of the above

15. Varicose veins are 15.____

A. mostly a cosmetic problem
B. related to venous valvular incompetence
C. treated successfully with elastic stocking sclero-therapy or vein stripping
D. all of the above

16. The risk of infection in surgical patients can be DECREASED by 16.____

A. limiting conversation in the operating room
B. a 5 minute initial scrub of operative team hands
C. use of paper drapes
D. all of the above

17. Polio, measles, and mumps are vaccines that contain live viruses and should NOT be given to patients who 17.____

A. are pregnant
B. are receiving chemotherapy
C. have AIDS
D. all of the above

18. CONTRAINDICATIONS for vaccination include 18.____

I. fever
II. progressive neurologic disorder
III. history of seizures

The CORRECT answer is:

A. I, II, III
B. II, III
C. I, III
D. II *only*

19. Symptoms of meningitis in newborns include 19.____

A. poor feeding
B. lethargy
C. bulging or full fontanel
D. all of the above

20. Which of the following should be provided to a breastfed infant? 20.____

A. Vitamin A
B. Vitamin D
C. Calcium
D. Iron

21. While on rounds at the newborn nursery, you are called in to see a 12 hour old infant who has begun convulsing. The FIRST line of treatment in this case would be 21.____

A. calcium gluconate
B. IV glucose
C. IV vitamin B_6
D. IV valium

22. While performing a physical examination on a newborn infant, you notice simian creases, epicanthal folds, and a heart murmur. 22.____
Your PRELIMINARY diagnosis would be

A. fetal alcohol syndrome
B. Down's syndrome
C. Turner's syndrome
D. tetralogy of Fallot

23. Asthma, which is the spasm of smooth muscle with intra-luminal collection of mucus and edema of mucus membranes, is associated with 23.____

A. eosinophilia
B. allergic rhinitis
C. atopic dermatitis
D. all of the above

24. Signs and symptoms of tuberculosis include 24.____

A. night sweats
B. failure to thrive
C. persistent cough
D. all of the above

25. Which of the following seizures is found EXCLUSIVELY in children and involve loss of consciousness and staring or eye fluttering, but no other motor involvement? 25.____

A. Partial complex
B. Tonic clonic
C. Absence (petit mal)
D. Partial simple

KEY (CORRECT ANSWERS)

1. A
2. B
3. A
4. C
5. C
6. C
7. B
8. D
9. D
10. D
11. C
12. B
13. A
14. C
15. D
16. D
17. D
18. A
19. D
20. B
21. B
22. B
23. D
24. D
25. C

EXAMINATION SECTION
TEST 1

DIRECTIONS: Each question or incomplete statement is followed by several suggested answers or completions. Select the one that BEST answers the question or completes the statement. *PRINT THE LETTER OF THE CORRECT ANSWER IN THE SPACE AT THE RIGHT.*

1. A 16-year-old boy suffers from a seizure disorder of the tonic clonic type. Which of the following drugs should be recommended for this patient? 1.____

   A. Ethosuximide
   B. Phenytoin
   C. Valium
   D. Valproic acid

2. A CT scan would prove helpful in making a diagnosis in a condition of 2.____

   A. persistent vomiting preceded by headache
   B. papilledema
   C. a neurologic abnormality
   D. all of the above

3. A newborn does not pass meconium within 24 hours, does not eat well, and has a distended abdomen with vomiting. 3.____
   The MOST probable diagnosis is

   A. pyloric stenosis
   B. anal fissures
   C. Hirschsprung's disease
   D. constipation

4. All of the following statements are true regarding congenital syphilis EXCEPT: 4.____

   A. Diagnosis includes a VDRL and FTA on CNS fluid
   B. The disease is usually spread during the birth process
   C. The disease is spread via the placenta
   D. Jaundice corresponds to the direct portion of bili-rubin

5. A 15-month-old child is on a trip to Mexico with his parents. The child begins to have diarrhea and diminished appetite. The parents had diarrhea too, but recovered by the time they came to the doctor. 5.____
   The MOST common cause of traveler's diarrhea is

   A. E. coli
   B. compylobacter jejuni
   C. shigella
   D. salmonella

6. A 4-year-old male child has a 2 month history of fatigue and intermittent fever. He appears pale, has aching joints, and his liver and spleen are enlarged and palpable. A CBC shows white blood cell count of 3000, Hb 8, hemato-crit 24.1, and thrombocytopenia. 6.____
   You would suspect

   A. brain tumor
   B. juvenile arthritis
   C. leukemia
   D. SLE

7. Causes of gynecomastia include 7.____

   A. puberty
   B. thyroid disorders
   C. malignancy
   D. all of the above

8. Which of the following drugs causes gynecomastia in patients who take it for a long time? 8.____

   A. Spironolactone
   B. Marijuana
   C. Phenothiazines
   D. All of the above

9. Enuresis is a common childhood problem with which parents must deal. Usually, children with enuresis have a reduced functional capacity bladder and are 3 years old before they can have full control of their bladder function. 9.____
   An enuretic child would be MOST helped by

   A. scolding and beating
   B. embarrassing the child in front of everyone
   C. behavior modification and training during the day with a reward
   D. making him wear diapers all the time

10. A 19-year-old girl is brought in by her mother. She is amenorrheic, has lost more than 25% of her body weight, and does not like to eat. The girl has an intense fear of being overweight. She does not want to be like her neighbor, who is very fat. 10.____
    What is the MOST probable diagnosis?

    A. Hyperthyroidism
    B. Anorexia nervosa
    C. Bulimia
    D. Diabetes mellitus

11. Which of the following statements is TRUE regarding spina bifida? 11.____

    A. The lesion is usually located in the lumbo sacral area of the spine
    B. It is often associated with dermal sinuses, dimples, and lipomas
    C. This can be detected prenatally by measuring alpha-fetoprotein in either maternal blood or amniotic fluid
    D. All of the above

12. A 3-year-old child is brought to your office by her mother. The child has itchy eyes and a purulent discharge with matting of the eyelids. 12.____
    The MOST likely diagnosis is ______ conjunctivitis.

    A. viral
    B. bacterial
    C. allergic
    D. herpetic

13. The treatment of choice for opthalmic neonatorum caused by chlamydia is 13.____

    A. erythromycin ointment
    B. penicillin G intramuscularly
    C. amoxicillin drops
    D. bactrim suspension

14. Signs of congenital dislocation of the hip joint include 14.____

    A. inability of the infant to bring himself to a standing position
    B. hip click or thump with manipulation of the hip joint
    C. frequent falling or loss of leg control
    D. all of the above

15. In order to protect a child from hepatitis B, the child should receive 15.____

    A. hepatitis B immunoglobulin at birth
    B. hepatitis B vaccine within 12 hours of birth
    C. booster at 1 and 6 months of age
    D. all of the above

16. The MOST common cause of diarrhea in children at day care centers i 16.____

A. giardia
B. E. coli
C. shigella
D. rota virus

17. ______ is a risk factor for coronary artery disease. 17.____

A. Smoking
B. Elevated cholesterol
C. Hypertension
D. All of the above

18. Which of the following is characteristic of giant hairy nevi? 18.____

A. Usually present at birth
B. Associated with malignant melanoma
C. Total removal recommended to reduce chance of cancer
D. All of the above

19. Cutaneous manifestations of SLE include 19.____

A. alopecia aereata
B. Wickam's striae on wrist and ankles
C. scalded skin on mouth and genitals
D. pruritis on dorsum of hand and feet

20. A 23-year-old male comes in with erythematous plaques with shiny, silvery, mica-like scales which are not pruritic and also involve the nails. 20.____
The MOST likely diagnosis is

A. ichthyosis
B. psoriasis
C. Reiter's syndrome
D. lichen planus

21. A patient comes in with erythematous, silvery, scaled plaques and hyperkeratolic papules of the palms and soles, frequently involving the mouth and genitals as well as the elbows, knees, and scalp. 21.____
What would be the MOST likely diagnosis?

A. Reiter's syndrome
B. Lupus erythematosis
C. Food allergy
D. Psoriasis

22. The etiology for urticaria is 22.____

I. food allergy
II. stress
III. drugs

The CORRECT answer is:

A. I, II
B. I, III
C. I, II, III
D. II, III

23. Complications of gastroesophageal reflux include 23.____

A. esophageal ulcer
B. esophageal stricture
C. pulmonary aspiration
D. all of the above

24. Acute gastritis is caused by 24.____

A. sepsis
B. NSAID
C. streptococcus and compylobacter infection
D. all of the above

25. A 45-year-old man, with no prior history of abdominal pain, has an episode of hematemesis. 25.____
This is MOST likely due to

A. esophageal varices
B. peptic ulcer
C. pulmonary tuberculosis
D. reflux esophagitis

KEY (CORRECT ANSWERS)

1. B
2. D
3. C
4. B
5. A

6. C
7. D
8. D
9. C
10. B

11. D
12. B
13. A
14. B
15. D

16. A
17. D
18. D
19. A
20. B

21. A
22. C
23. D
24. D
25. A

TEST 2

DIRECTIONS: Each question or incomplete statement is followed by several suggested answers or completions. Select the one that BEST answers the question or completes the statement. *PRINT THE LETTER OF THE CORRECT ANSWER IN THE SPACE AT THE RIGHT.*

1. Which of the following drugs causes liver toxicity? 1.____

   A. INH
   B. Acetaminophen
   C. Chlorpromazine
   D. All of the above

2. In order to investigate the cause of bleeding from the large bowel in a 70-year-old woman, the procedure of choice would be 2.____

   A. angiography
   B. barium studies
   C. proctosigmoidoscopy
   D. fiberoptic endoscope

3. A 42-year-old man comes in with intermittent epigastric burning pain. According to him, this pain is usually relieved with food or antacid. 3.____
   The MOST likely diagnosis is

   A. Crohn's disease
   B. acute pancreatitis
   C. peptic ulcer
   D. acute cholecystitis

4. A 34-year-old female comes in with the complaint of right upper abdominal pain, which increases gradually in severity. It refers to the back, and the pain occurs at the level of the scapula. 4.____
   You would suspect

   A. acute pancreatitis
   B. acute cholecystitis
   C. acute bowel obstruction
   D. dissecting aortic aneurysm

5. Symptoms of irritable bowel syndrome include 5.____

   A. abdominal discomfort
   B. alterations of bowel habit
   C. lack of organic cause
   D. all of the above

6. The test FTA-ABS 6.____

   A. is a fluorescent test that detects antibodies found in response to causative agent T pallidum
   B. is specific for syphilis
   C. has no false positive results
   D. all of the above

7. A female patient complains of vaginal irritation, thick, grayish-white watery discharge with a fishy odor, and shedding of vaginal squamous epithelial cells. 7.____
   The MOST likely diagnosis is

   A. chlamydia trachomatis
   B. trichomonas vaginalis
   C. gardnerella
   D. C. albicans

8. A 22-year-old female patient complains of greenish vaginal discharge and vaginal irritation accompanied by strawberry spots on the vaginal epithelium. 8.____
The PROBABLE diagnosis is

A. trichomonas vaginalis
B. gonorrhea
C. albicans
D. herpes hominis

9. A female patient asks you the best time during the menstrual cycle to check for masses in the breast by self-examination. 9.____
You should tell her that the BEST time for self-examination is

A. 4-5 days before menses
B. 2-3 days after menses
C. during menstruation
D. at the time of ovulation

10. Cyanosis and softening of the cervix in the beginning of pregnancy are called ______ sign. 10.____

A. Hegar's
B. Goodell's
C. Ladin's
D. McDonald's

11. By using ultrasound, fetal heart tones can be FIRST detected at day 11.____

A. 15
B. 28
C. 44
D. 57

12. The second stage of labor involves the time period 12.____

A. from complete dilatation of the cervix to the delivery of the infant
B. from delivery of the infant to delivery of the placenta
C. of the first hour after delivery
D. none of the above

13. The Apgar score is based on one minute and 5 minute evaluations. 13.____
Its components include

A. respiration
B. appearance
C. tone
D. all of the above

14. A female in her 18th week of pregnancy complains of bleeding, cramping, dilated cervix, and ruptured membranes, but no passage of tissue. 14.____
What is the MOST likely diagnosis? ______ abortion.

A. Threatened
B. Inevitable
C. Missed
D. None of the above

15. A patient is in the latter part of her first trimester. On examination, her uterus is not growing according to gestational age. On ultrasound, no fetal heart sound is heard. 15.____
The MOST likely diagnosis is ______ abortion.

A. missed
B. incomplete
C. habitual
D. complete

16. Cigarette smoking during pregnancy 16.____

A. has its greatest influence during the last 4 months of pregnancy
B. results in decreased weight of the infant
C. results in decreased length and head circumference of the infant
D. all of the above

17. A female, 7 months pregnant, was involved in a high impact motor vehicle accident. She suffered vaginal bleeding, absent fetal heart tones, and shock. The treatment of choice should be 17.____

A. normal vaginal delivery
B. cesarean section
C. continuation of pregnancy up to the end
D. bedrest

18. The normal baseline FHR is ______ bpm. 18.____

A. 140
B. 90
C. 180
D. none of the above

19. Ritodrine hydrochloride is the only FDA approved tocoly-tic agent used in premature labor. Its side effects include 19.____

A. hypotension
B. tachycardia
C. pulmonary edema
D. all of the above

20. A fetus that is delivered before 38 weeks gestation is considered 20.____

A. postmature
B. premature
C. term fetus
D. postdate

21. The fetal position in which the hips are flexed and the knees extended so that the legs come to lie alongside the fetal head is called a ______ presentation. 21.____

A. incomplete breech
B. full breech
C. frank breech
D. double footling

22. ______ should be INCREASED in pregnant and lactating women. 22.____

A. Vitamin B_{12}
B. Iron
C. Magnesium
D. Phosphate

23. The MOST common cause of spontaneous abortion in the first trimester is 23.____

A. incompetent cervix
B. infection
C. abnormal product of conception
D. uterine dysfunction

24. The AVERAGE amount of blood lost in a typical menstrual cycle is ______ ml. 24.____

A. 20
B. 10
C. 30
D. 80

25. A 32-year-old female experiences abnormal uterine bleeding. The BEST diagnostic procedure to determine the cause of her bleeding would be a(n) 25.____

A. D & E
B. D & C
C. hysteroscopy
D. laproscopy

KEY (CORRECT ANSWERS)

1. D
2. C
3. C
4. B
5. D

6. D
7. C
8. A
9. B
10. B

11. C
12. A
13. D
14. B
15. A

16. D
17. B
18. A
19. D
20. B

21. C
22. B
23. C
24. C
25. B

EXAMINATION SECTION
TEST 1

DIRECTIONS: Each question or incomplete statement is followed by several suggested answers or completions. Select the one that BEST answers the question or completes the statement. *PRINT THE LETTER OF THE CORRECT ANSWER IN THE SPACE AT THE RIGHT.*

1. A 32-year-old female comes to the office with itchy areas around the nipple of her right breast. Upon examination, you notice nipple and aerolar erosion and a weeping eczemoid lesion. The MOST likely diagnosis is 1.____

   A. Paget's disease
   B. breast carcinoma
   C. breast abscess
   D. none of the above

2. A 23-year-old female patient comes to you complaining of bleeding between periods. This is called 2.____

   A. hypermenorrhea
   B. metrorrhagia
   C. polymenorrhea
   D. oligomenorrhea

3. The term oligomenorrhea is used to describe 3.____

   A. scanty periods
   B. heavy bleeding
   C. infrequent periods
   D. prolonged bleeding

4. Risk factors for the development of cervical cancer include 4.____

   A. sexual intercourse at an early age
   B. multiple partners
   C. high parity
   D. all of the above

5. Secondary dysmenorrhea can be caused by 5.____

   A. endometriosis
   B. uterine polyps
   C. an ovarian cyst
   D. all of the above

6. Danazol, the drug used in the treatment of endometriosis, 6.____

   A. is very cheap
   B. has no side effects
   C. has a masculinizing effect on female fetuses
   D. all of the above

7. All of the following are signs and symptoms of endometriosis EXCEPT 7.____

   A. dysmenorrhea
   B. dyspareunia
   C. amenorrhea
   D. low back pain

8. Stein-Levanthal syndrome is associated with all of the following EXCEPT 8.____

   A. menorrhagia
   B. oligomenorrhea
   C. infertility
   D. anovulation

9. Of the following procedures, the one that can be performed SAFELY on a pregnant patient is a(n) 9.____

A. endometrial biopsy
B. culdocentesis
C. hysteroscopy
D. none of the above

10. According to Nageles rule, which of the following calculations is CORRECT for estimated date of confinement? _______ day of last menstrual period plus _______. 10.____

A. First; 9 months + 7 days
B. Last; 7 days
C. First; 7 months
D. Last; 8 months

11. A 36-year-old pregnant female comes to the office. She is worried about the health of the fetus because of her age. The doctor advises an amniocentesis.
Of which of the following risk factors associated with amniocentesis should she be aware? 11.____

A. Maternal infection
B. Hemorrhage
C. Premature labor
D. All of the above

12. A 24-year-old female patient suffers from lower right abdominal pain, nausea, and weakness. Her last menstrual period was ten weeks ago. She is afebrile and shows tenderness on pelvic examination.
The MOST likely diagnosis is 12.____

A. PID
B. threatened abortion
C. ectopic pregnancy
D. missed abortion

13. Pregnant women with diabetes are at risk for 13.____

A. babies with hydramnios
B. large babies
C. stillbirths
D. all of the above

14. Use of _______ supresses lactation. 14.____

A. diethyl stilbesterol
B. bromocriptine
C. ethynyl estradiol
D. all of the above

15. The prevention of diseases before they occur by controlling risk factors through immunization, genetic counseling, and environmental control measures is referred to as 15.____

A. health risk analysis
B. primary prevention
C. well care
D. secondary prevention

16. Which of the following has been associated with physical inactivity? 16.____

A. Coronary artery disease
B. Hypertension
C. Diabetes
D. All of the above

17. A 65-year-old man comes into the office with complaints of easy fatigability and weakness in the extraocular muscles with ptosis and diplopia. Examination reveals proximal arm muscle weakness.
The MOST likely diagnosis is 17.____

A. muscular dystrophy
B. myasthenia gravis
C. polymyositis
D. multiple sclerosis

18. Clinical features of Parkinson's disease include 18.____

    A. slowness of movement
    B. fixed facial expression
    C. tremor pronounced at rest
    D. all of the above

19. A 38-year-old patient has a single thyroid nodule, enlarged lymph nodes, and a remote history of neck irradiation. 19.____
    What is the MOST likely diagnosis?

    A. Thyroid carcinoma
    B. Benign thyroid nodule
    C. Thyroiditis
    D. Follicular adenoma

20. A 23-year-old diabetic takes insulin at 20 NPH and 7 regular units. Her FBS level is usually 90-110 mg/dl. However, late in the afternoon she becomes very irritable and sometimes gets headaches. 20.____
    The BEST treatment would be

    A. adding 5 units of regular insulin before dinner
    B. increasing regular insulin in the morning
    C. adding a midafternoon snack
    D. taking aspirin for headaches

21. Among the risk factors for development of osteoporosis is 21.____

    A. good regular exercise
    B. male gender
    C. female gender
    D. black race

22. Deficiency of vitamin ______ causes osteomalacia. 22.____

    A. A
    B. D
    C. C
    D. E

23. Long-term treatment with glucocorticosteroids may produce side effects, including 23.____

    A. myopathics
    B. fat redistribution
    C. osteoporosis
    D. all of the above

24. A 6-year-old boy is brought in by his mother because his eye is red and he keeps rubbing it. He feels something in his eye. 24.____
    What should you use to remove the foreign body?

    A. Normal saline high pressure irrigation
    B. Fine gauge needle
    C. Cotton tip applicator
    D. Burr tip

25. A 5-year-old ingested an unknown quantity of aspirin. The child is alert. The child's father is on the phone with you and tells you that the emergency room is 30 minutes away from their home. 25.____
    You should tell the child's father to

    A. do nothing until they reach the emergency room
    B. induce vomiting
    C. ask the child to drink glucose water
    D. have the child drink as much milk as possible

KEY (CORRECT ANSWERS)

1. A
2. B
3. C
4. D
5. D
6. C
7. C
8. A
9. B
10. A
11. D
12. C
13. D
14. D
15. B
16. D
17. B
18. D
19. A
20. C
21. C
22. B
23. D
24. B
25. B

TEST 2

DIRECTIONS: Each question or incomplete statement is followed by several suggested answers or completions. Select the one that BEST answers the question or completes the statement. *PRINT THE LETTER OF THE CORRECT ANSWER IN THE SPACE AT THE RIGHT.*

Questions 1-4.

DIRECTIONS: In Questions 1 through 4, match the numbered poisonous substance with the lettered breath odor, listed in the column below, that it produces.

A. Garlic
B. Pears
C. Bitter almond
D. Rotten eggs

1. Arsenic 1.____
2. Cyanide 2.____
3. Hydrogen sulphide 3.____
4. Chloral hydrate 4.____

Questions 5-10.

DIRECTIONS: In Questions 5 through 10, match the numbered characteristic with the lettered disorder, listed in the column below, with which it is MOST closely associated.

A. Rheumatoid arthritis
B. Osteoarthritis
C. SLE
D. Ankylosing spondolytis
E. Gout

5. Bilateral symmetrical polyarthritis 5.____
6. Accompanied by inflammatory bowel disease mostly in males 6.____
7. Joint pain that worsens with activity 7.____
8. Results from repetitive occupational activity 8.____
9. Mucosal ulcerations of nose and mouth 9.____
10. Explosive onset 10.____

Questions 11-15.

DIRECTIONS: In Questions 11 through 15, mark:

A. if the described characteristic is associated with DELIRIUM
B. if the described characteristic is associated with DEMENTIA
C. if the described characteristic is associated with BOTH delirium and dementia
D. if the described characteristic is associated with NEITHER delirium nor dementia

11. Attention and alertness usually normal 11.____

12. Orientation often impaired 12.____

13. Visual hallucinations are common 13.____

14. Onset insidious rather than acute 14.____

15. Little or no memory impairment 15.____

Questions 16-20.

DIRECTIONS: In Questions 16 through 20, match the numbered function or effect with the lettered drug, listed in the column below, which performs that function or produces that effect.

A. Heroin
B. Marijuana
C. PCP
D. Naloxone
E. Cocaine

16. Preferred treatment for opiate 16.____

17. Widely used mind-altering drug 17.____

18. Produces distortion of body image 18.____

19. Topical anesthetic used in eye 19.____

20. Clonidine is used to ameliorate withdrawal 20.____

Questions 21-25.

DIRECTIONS: In Questions 21 through 25, match the numbered condition with the lettered menstrual disorder, listed in the column below, that it BEST defines.

A. Menorrhagia
B. Amenorrhea
C. Polymenorrhea
D. Oligomenorrhea
E. Metrorrhagia

21. Frequent periods 21.____

22. Absent periods 22.____

23. Heavy bleeding 23.____

24. Infrequent periods 24.____

25. Bleeding between periods 25.____

KEY (CORRECT ANSWERS)

1.	A	11.	B
2.	C	12.	C
3.	D	13.	A
4.	B	14.	B
5.	A	15.	D
6.	D	16.	D
7.	B	17.	B
8.	B	18.	C
9.	C	19.	E
10.	E	20.	A

21. C
22. B
23. A
24. D
25. E

EXAMINATION SECTION
TEST 1

DIRECTIONS: Each question or incomplete statement is followed by several suggested answers or completions. Select the one that BEST answers the question or completes the statement. *PRINT THE LETTER OF THE CORRECT ANSWER IN THE SPACE AT THE RIGHT.*

Questions 1-10.

DIRECTIONS: Questions 1 through 10 are to be answered on the basis of the following information.

Ms. Martha McCarthy, 32 years old, is brought to the emergency unit on a stretcher. Ms. McCarthy was in an automobile accident and is conscious upon admission. X-rays show that she has considerable vertebral damage at the level of T-6. The surgical unit is notified that Ms. McCarthy will be brought directly from the x-ray department.

1. Which of the facts about Ms. McCarthy, if obtained when she is admitted to the hospital, would MOST likely require early intervention? She 1.____

   A. is a vegetarian
   B. last voided 7 hours ago
   C. smokes 2 packs of cigarettes a day
   D. is menstruating

2. Twelve hours after admission, Ms. McCarthy begins to develop some difficulty in breathing. In addition to obtaining a respirator and calling the physician, the nurse would show the BEST judgment by 2.____

   A. turning Ms. McCarthy onto her abdomen to promote drainage from the mouth and throat
   B. encouraging Ms. McCarthy to exercise her upper extremities at intervals
   C. elevating the foot of Ms. McCarthy's bed
   D. bringing pharyngeal suction equipment to Ms. McCarthy's bedside

3. Considering the level of Ms. McCarthy's injury (T-6), it is MOST justifiable to assume that her respiratory difficulty is due to 3.____

   A. edema of the cord above the level of injury
   B. hemorrhage into the brain stem due to trauma
   C. movement of the parts of the fractured vertebrae
   D. severing of the nerves that activate the diaphragm

4. The nurse can prevent Ms. McCarthy's lower extremities from rotating externally by placing 4.____

   A. her feet against a footboard
   B. pillows against her calves

C. trochanter rolls along the inner aspects of her knees
D. sandbags against the outer aspects of her thighs

5. Ms. McCarthy is to have a laminectomy. 5.____
The CHIEF purpose of a laminectomy for her is to

A. realign the vertebral fragments
B. relieve pressure on the cord
C. repair spinal nerve damage
D. reduce spinal fluid pressure

6. Ms. McCarthy is highly susceptible to the development of decubitus ulcers because 6.____

A. an intact nervous system is necessary for maintenance of normal tone of blood vessels
B. flexor muscles have a greater loss of tone than extensor muscles
C. decreased permeability of the capillary walls results from central nervous system damage
D. atonic muscles have an increased need for oxygen

7. Ms. McCarthy has a laminectomy and spinal fusion. The physician tells her that she will not be able to walk without the use of supportive devices. 7.____
Before surgery, Ms. McCarthy should have been informed that the bone to be used as a graft for a spinal fusion is MOST likely to be obtained from the

A. posterior iliac crest
B. adjacent sacral vertebrae
C. humerus
D. sternum

8. The nursing staff notices a pronounced change in Ms. McCarthy's behavior after the physician discusses her prognosis with her. She is now overtly rebellious, responding negatively to personnel, to treatments, and to nursing measures. 8.____
The interpretation of her behavior is that she is

A. unable to face the prospect of a long rehabilitative program
B. projecting her own unhappiness onto others
C. reacting to the change in her body image
D. seeking punishment for feelings of guilt about her injury

9. A rehabilitative program is started for Ms. McCarthy. She is to wear leg braces. 9.____
When applying Ms. McCarthy's leg braces, it is ESSENTIAL for the nurse to consider that Ms. McCarthy

A. cannot move her lower extremities
B. has no sensation in her lower extremities
C. can flex her knees to a 45-degree angle
D. cannot fully extend her hip joints

10. To achieve success in a rehabilitation program for Ms. McCarthy, the MOST important information about Ms. McCarthy is her 10.____

A. knowledge of services available to her
B. personal goals
C. being encouraged by her family
D. relationship with members of the health team

Questions 11-16.

DIRECTIONS: Questions 11 through 16 are to be answered on the basis of the following information.

Ms. Beth Marks, a 21-year-old college student, sustains a head injury as a result of a fall down a flight of stairs. She is brought to the emergency room with a pronounced swelling of the forehead. She is admitted to the hospital for observation.

11. On admission, Ms. Marks' blood pressure was 110/80, her pulse rate was 88, and her respiratory rate was 20. 11.____
It would be MOST indicative of increasing intracranial pressure if her blood pressure, pulse, and respirations were, respectively,

A. 90/54; 50; 22
B. 100/66; 120; 32
C. 120/90; 96; 16
D. 140/70; 60; 14

12. Ms. Marks' condition worsens. She has a craniotomy, and a hematoma is removed. Her postoperative orders include elevation of the head of her bed, and mannitol. 12.____
When Ms. Marks reacts from anesthesia, she is put in a semi-reclining position to

A. increase thoracic expansion and facilitate oxygenation of damaged tissue
B. provide adequate drainage and prevent fluid accumulation in the cranial cavity
C. decrease cardiac workload and prevent hemorrhage at the surgical site
D. reduce pressure in the subarachnoid space and promote tissue granulation

13. It is CORRECT to say that in this case mannitol is expected to 13.____

A. decrease body fluids
B. elevate the filtration rate in the kidney
C. control filtration of nitrogenous wastes
D. increase the volume of urine

14. The PRIMARY purpose of administering mannitol to Ms. Marks is to 14.____

A. promote kidney function
B. prevent bladder distention
C. reduce cerebral pressure
D. diminish peripheral fluid retention

15. Eight hours after surgery, Ms. Marks' temperature rises to 104° F. (40° C.), and a hypothermia blanket is ordered for her. 15.____
Ms. Marks' temperature elevation is MOST likely due to a(n)

A. accumulation of respiratory secretions resulting from inadequate ventilation
B. alteration of metabolism resulting from pressure on the hypothalamus
C. increase in leukocytosis resulting from bacterial invasion
D. constriction of the main artery in the circle of Willis resulting from a ventricular fluid shift

16. Following a craniotomy, a patient may be given caffeine and sodium benzoate to 16.____

A. lessen cerebral irritation by depressing the cerebrum
B. improve the sense of touch by blocking spinal nerve reflexes

C. enable commands to be followed by activating the medullary cells
D. increase mental alertness by stimulating the cerebral cortex

Questions 17-25.

DIRECTIONS: Questions 17 through 25 are to be answered on the basis of the following information.

Mr. Paul Peters, 61 years old, is admitted to the hospital. Vascular occlusion of his left leg is suspected, and he is scheduled for an arteriogram.

17. The nurse is to assess the circulation in Mr. Peters' lower extremities. Which of these measures would be ESPECIALLY significant? 17.____

A. Comparing the pulses in the lower extremities
B. Comparing the temperatures of the lower extremities
C. Noting the pulse in the left leg
D. Noting the temperature of the left leg

18. Which of these symptoms manifested in Mr. Peters' affected left extremity would indicate that he has intermittent claudication? 18.____

A. Extensive discoloration
B. Dependent edema
C. Pain associated with activity
D. Petechiae

19. Following Mr. Peters' admission, an IMMEDIATE goal in his care should be to 19.____

A. improve the muscular strength of his extremities
B. achieve maximum rehabilitation for him
C. prevent the extension of his disease process
D. protect his extremities from injury

20. During the night following his admission, Mr. Peters says that he can't sleep because his feet are cold.
The nurse should 20.____

A. offer Mr. Peters a warm drink
B. massage Mr. Peters' feet briskly for several minutes
C. ask Mr. Peters if he has any socks with him
D. place a heating pad under Mr. Peters' feet

21. Information given to Mr. Peters about the femoral arteri-ogram should include the fact that 21.____

A. a local anesthetic will be given to lessen discomfort
B. there are minimal risks associated with the procedure
C. the radioactive dye that is injected will be removed before he returns to his unit
D. a radiopaque substance will be injected directly into the small vessels of his feet

22. When Mr. Peters is brought back to his unit following the arteriogram, which of these actions would be appropriate? 22.____

A. Encourage fluid intake and have him lie prone
B. Apply heat to the site used for introducing the intravenous catheter and passively exercise his involved extremity
C. Limit motion of his affected extremity and check the site used for the injection of the dye
D. Restrict his fluid intake and encourage him to ambulate

23. The results of Mr. Peters' arteriogram revealed a marked narrowing of the left femoral artery. He has a venous graft bypass performed. Following a stay in the recovery room, he is returned to his room. 23.____
The postoperative care plan for Mr. Peters should include which of these notations?

A. Keep the affected extremity elevated
B. Check the pulse distal to the graft site
C. Check for color changes proximal to the proximal site
D. Check for fine movements of the toes

24. During the first postoperative day, Mr. Peters is kept on bed rest. 24.____
Which of these exercises for Mr. Peters would it be APPROPRIATE for the nurse to initiate?

A. Straight leg raising of both lower extremities
B. Range of motion of both lower extremities
C. Abduction of the affected extremity
D. Dorsiflexion and extension of the foot of the affected extremity

25. When Mr. Peters returns to bed after ambulating, it would be MOST important for the nurse to check 25.____

A. his blood pressure
B. his radial pulse
C. the temperature of his affected extremity
D. the pedal pulse of his affected extremity

KEY (CORRECT ANSWERS)

1. B
2. D
3. A
4. D
5. B
6. A
7. A
8. C
9. B
10. B
11. D
12. B
13. D
14. C
15. B
16. D
17. A
18. C
19. D
20. C
21. A
22. C
23. B
24. D
25. D

TEST 2

DIRECTIONS: Each question or incomplete statement is followed by several suggested answers or completions. Select the one that BEST answers the question or completes the statement. *PRINT THE LETTER OF THE CORRECT ANSWER IN THE SPACE AT THE RIGHT.*

Questions 1-8.

DIRECTIONS: Questions 1 through 8 are to be answered on the basis of the following information.

Three days ago, Susan Cooper, 4 years old, was admitted to the hospital with a diagnosis of heart failure. She was digitalized the day of her admission and is now to receive a maintenance dose of digoxin (Lanoxin) 0.08 mg. p.o.b.i.d. Susan has been under medical supervision for cystic fibrosis and has severe pulmonary involvement.

1. The stock bottle of Lanoxin contains 0.05 mg. of the drug in 1 cc. of solution. How much solution will contain a single dose (0.08 mg.) of the drug for Susan? _______ cc. 1.____

   A. 0.06 B. 0.6 C. 1.6 D. 2.6

2. Prior to the administration of a dose of Lanoxin to Susan, the nurse should take her _______ pulse. 2.____

   A. femoral
   B. apical
   C. radial
   D. both apical and radial

3. The nurse would be CORRECT in withholding Susan's dose of Lanoxin without specific instructions from the doctor if Susan's pulse rate were below beats per minute. 3.____

   A. 100 B. 115 C. 130 D. 145

4. Which of these measures is likely to be MOST helpful in providing for Susan's nutritional needs while she is acutely ill? 4.____

   A. Serving her food lukewarm
   B. Giving her only liquids that she can take through a straw
   C. Offering her small portions of favorite foods frequently
   D. Mixing her foods together so that they are not readily identifiable

5. Because Susan has symptoms of acute cardiac failure, her oral feedings will DIFFER from the feedings of a normal child the same age in the 5.____

   A. size of the feedings *only*
   B. rapidity and size of the feedings
   C. frequency and rapidity of the feedings
   D. size, rapidity, and frequency of the feedings

6. All of the following information is part of Susan's health history. Which fact relates MOST directly to a diagnosis of cystic fibrosis? 6.____

   A. Emergency surgery as a newborn for intestinal obstruction
   B. Jaundice that lasted 4 days during the newborn period

C. A temperature of 104° F. (40° C.) followed by a convulsion when she was 6 months old
D. A left otitis media treated with antibiotics when she was 12 months old

7. Susan is placed in a mist tent in order to 7.____

A. increase the hydration of secretions
B. prevent the loss of fluids through evaporation
C. aid in maintaining a therapeutic environmental temperature
D. improve the transport of oxygen and carbon dioxide

8. Susan is receiving pancreatin replacement therapy to promote the absorption of 8.____

A. protein
B. carbohydrate
C. vitamin C (ascorbic acid)
D. sodium

Questions 9-13.

DIRECTIONS: Questions 9 through 13 are to be answered on the basis of the following information.

Ms. Leslie Browne, a 21-year-old college student, is seen by a physician because of fatigue and weight loss. Physical examination reveals slight enlargement of her cervical lymph nodes. Ms. Browne is admitted to the hospital for diagnostic studies.

9. Ms. Browne states that she has had a low-grade fever. Which of these questions pertaining to Ms. Browne's low-grade fever should the nurse ask INITIALLY? 9.____

A. When did you first notice that your temperature had gone up?
B. Has your temperature been over 102 degrees?
C. Have you recently been exposed to anyone who has an infection?
D. Do you have a sore throat?

10. Ms. Browne is to have a chest x-ray and is to be transported to the x-ray department by stretcher. All of the following actions may be taken by the nurse when sending Ms. Browne for the x-ray. Which action is ESSENTIAL? 10.____

A. Strap Ms. Browne securely to the stretcher.
B. Place Ms. Browne's chart under the mattress of the stretcher.
C. Ask Ms. Browne to remove her wristwatch.
D. Assign a nurse's aide to accompany Ms. Browne.

11. The results of diagnostic tests establish that Ms. Browne has Hodgkin's disease with involvement of the cervical and mediastinal nodes. She is to have an initial course of intravenous chemotherapy with mechlorethamine (Mustar-gen) hydrochloride. The Mustargen that Ms. Browne receives is administered to her through the tubing of a rapidly flowing intravenous infusion.
The purpose of this method of administration is to 11.____

A. reduce the half-life of the medication
B. minimize the side effects of the medication

C. decrease irritation of the blood vessel by the medication
D. control the rate of absorption of the medication

12. While Ms. Browne is receiving Mustargen therapy, she is MOST likely to develop 12.____

A. alopecia
B. fecal impactions
C. temporary neuropathy
D. transient nausea

13. The insertion site of Ms. Browne's intravenous infusion is edematous. Which of these actions should the nurse take? 13.____

A. Lower the height of the infusion container
B. Discontinue the infusion
C. Flush the infusion tubing with 5 ml. of isotonic saline solution
D. Reduce the rate of infusion

Questions 14-25.

DIRECTIONS: Questions 14 through 25 are to be answered on the basis of the following information.

Mr. Robert Dine, a 66-year-old widower who has diabetes mellitus, is admitted to the hospital in metabolic acidosis. He has gangrene of the great toe of his left foot and ulceration of the heel.

14. Immediately after Mr. Dine's admission, the nurse places him on his side and then at frequent intervals turns him from side to side. The CHIEF purpose of these actions is to 14.____

A. reduce the possibility of pulmonary embolism
B. insure maximal circulation in the gangrenous extremity
C. promote the exchange of oxygen and carbon dioxide
D. facilitate the breakdown of lactic acid

15. Because Mr. Dine has a gangrenous toe and a heel ulcer, which of the following equipment is ESSENTIAL to his care? 15.____

A. Sheepskin pad
B. Heat lamp
C. Bed board
D. Cradle

16. The physician has ordered warm saline dressings to be applied to Mr. Dine's heel ulcer for 20 minutes twice a day. A nurse observes another staff nurse preparing a clean basin and a washcloth to carry out the treatment. Which of these approaches by the nurse who makes the observation would be APPROPRIATE? 16.____

A. Interrupt the nurse assembling supplies to discuss the procedure
B. Present the situation for discussion at a team conference
C. Do nothing, as the procedure is being done using correct technique
D. Do nothing, as each nurse is accountable for her or his own actions

17. Mr. Dine's lesions have not responded to conservative medical therapy. He is scheduled to have a below-the-knee amputation of the affected extremity. Mr. Dine's orders include administration of regular insulin on a sliding scale. Mr. Dine, who received isophane (NPH) insulin prior to his admission to the hospital, has been on regular insulin since admission. Regular insulin is to be continued for him until after his recovery from surgery. Mr. Dine asks what the reason is for this order. Which of the following information would give Mr. Dine the BEST explanation? 17.____

A. When complications are present, diabetes is more manageable with regular insulin.
B. During the first week after a patient recovers from an episode of diabetic acidosis, the likelihood of a recurrence is greatest.
C. Diminished activity intensifies the body's response to long-acting insulin.
D. Diabetic acidosis causes a temporary increase in the rate of food absorption.

18. Mr. Dine asks why he cannot be given insulin by mouth. He should be informed that insulin is NOT given by mouth because it 18.____

A. is destroyed by digestive enzymes
B. is irritating to the gastrointestinal tract
C. is detoxified by the liver
D. cannot be regulated as it is absorbed

19. Mr. Dine is receiving an intravenous infusion of 5% glucose in distilled water. Regular insulin is administered intravenously every two hours.
The purpose of the insulin is to 19.____

A. enhance carbohydrate metabolism
B. promote conversion of fat to glycogen
C. stimulate gluconeogenesis
D. assist in the regulation of fluid absorption

20. Regular insulin is given to Mr. Dine on a sliding scale to 20.____

A. lengthen its peak action
B. minimize the risk of hypoglycemia
C. prolong glyconeogenesis
D. prevent the rapid release of glucagon

21. Mr. Dine has a below-the-knee amputation. Following recovery from anesthesia, he is brought back to the surgical unit. Because Mr. Dine has diabetes mellitus, he is susceptible to the development of a wound infection postoperatively.
Mr. Dine's care plan should include measures that will overcome the fact that patients with diabetes mellitus have 21.____

A. ketone bodies excreted into their subcutaneous tissue
B. a greater insensitivity to antibiotics
C. decreased ability to combat pathogens
D. a larger number of microscopic organisms on their skin

22. To prevent the deformities to which Mr. Dine is particularly susceptible, his affected limb should be placed with the hip 22.____

    A. flexed and the knee extended
    B. rotated outwardly and the knee flexed
    C. extended and the knee flexed
    D. and knee extended

23. Mr. Dine's condition improves. Physical therapy treatments are begun for him. He is to be taught crutch-walking. After returning from his first treatment, Mr. Dine begins to cry. The nurse's attempts to explore with Mr. Dine the reasons for his crying have been unsuccessful. Under these circumstances, it would be justifiable for the nurse to proceed on the assumption that Mr. Dine's behavior is PROBABLY related to a 23.____

    A. fear of becoming dependent
    B. feeling of loss
    C. reaction to physical pain
    D. response to muscle reconditioning

24. Mr. Dine is now receiving a daily dose of a long-acting insulin preparation that he will continue to take at home. 24.____
    Which of these bedtime snacks would be BEST for him?

    A. Cheese and crackers
    B. An apple and diet cola
    C. Orange juice and toast
    D. Canned peaches and tea

25. Before Mr. Dine is discharged, he should have which of these understandings about his own care? 25.____

    A. Less insulin will be required since the diseased tissue has been removed.
    B. Social activities must be limited to conserve energy.
    C. The stump should be examined daily.
    D. Tissue breakdown will be prevented if foods high in vitamin C are taken daily.

KEY(CORRECT ANSWERS)

1. C
2. B
3. A
4. C
5. D
6. A
7. A
8. A
9. A
10. A
11. C
12. D
13. B
14. C
15. D
16. A
17. A
18. A
19. A
20. B
21. C
22. D
23. B
24. A
25. C

TEST 3

DIRECTIONS: Each question or incomplete statement is followed by several suggested answers or completions. Select the one that BEST answers the question or completes the statement. *PRINT THE LETTER OF THE CORRECT ANSWER IN THE SPACE AT THE RIGHT.*

1. A physician orders the following pre-operative medications for a child: Demerol hydrochloride 8 mg.; Atropine sulfate 0.06 mg. On hand are the following vials: Meperidine (Demerol) hydrochloride 50 mg. in 1 cc.; Atropine sulfate 0.40 mg. in 1 cc. In order to administer the prescribed doses, the nurse should give ______ of meperidine and ______ of atropine. 1.____

   A. 0.16 cc.; 0.15 cc.
   B. 0.26 cc.; 0.20 cc.
   C. 1 minim; 3 minims
   D. 2 minims; 4 minims

2. To provide care to a patient who has lost a body part or valued function, which of these measures is ESSENTIAL to include in the care plan? 2.____

   A. Inviting the assistance of a person who has a similar handicap
   B. Encouraging an immediate independence in self-care
   C. Providing information to the patient about available prosthetic devices
   D. Allowing adequate time for the patient to work through his grief

Questions 3-9.

DIRECTIONS: Questions 3 through 9 are to be answered on the basis of the following information.

Ms. Gloria Goldstein, 40 years old, visits a physician because of pain in her left leg. The physician determines that Ms. Goldstein has thrombophlebitis in her left leg and hospital admission is arranged. Her orders include bed rest and bishydroxycoumarin (Dicumarol).

3. Bed rest is prescribed for Ms. Goldstein in order to 3.____

   A. promote fluctuations in the venous pressure of both extremities
   B. improve the capacity of the venous circulation in both extremities
   C. minimize the potential for release of a thrombus in the affected extremity
   D. prevent thrombus formation in the unaffected extremity

4. The expected action of Dicumarol is to 4.____

   A. dissolve a thrombus
   B. prevent extension of a thrombus
   C. promote healing of the infarction
   D. reduce vascular necrosis

5. To detect a common untoward effect of Dicumarol, the nurse should assess Ms. Goldstein for the possible development of 5.____

   A. generalized dermatitis
   B. hematuria
   C. urinary retention
   D. vitamin K deficiency

6. While Ms. Goldstein is receiving Dicumarol, she should be monitored by which of these laboratory tests? 6.____

   A. Prothrombin time
   B. Clotting time
   C. Red cell fragility
   D. Platelet count

7. An order for which of these medications should be questioned because it is usually contraindicated for a patient receiving Dicumarol? 7.____

   A. Cortisone
   B. Aspirin
   C. Chlorpromazine hydrochloride (Thorazine)
   D. Isoproterenol (Isuprel) hydrochloride

8. The nurse is talking with Ms. Goldstein on the third day of her hospitalization. Suddenly, Ms. Goldstein, who is in bed, complains of a sharp pain in the left side of her chest. The physician establishes a diagnosis of pulmonary embolus. Ms. Goldstein's orders include absolute bed rest and heparin. 8.____
   Which of these medications should be readily available while Ms. Goldstein is receiving heparin therapy?

   A. Procainamide (Pronestyl) hydrochloride
   B. Protamine sulfate
   C. Papaverine hydrochloride
   D. Calcium gluconate

9. At lunchtime one day, Ms. Goldstein, who is on a regular diet, states that she does not feel hungry. 9.____
   The nurse should

   A. encourage her to eat the full meal
   B. emphasize her need for protein
   C. limit her snacks
   D. allow her to eat as she likes

10. The BEST beginning point in offering support to a patient in time of crisis is to 10.____

   A. tell the client what to do to solve the problem
   B. imply that the client is a competent person
   C. find a person or agency to take care of the problem
   D. remind the client that everyone has to cope with crises

Questions 11-16.

DIRECTIONS: Questions 11 through 16 are to be answered on the basis of the following information.

Ms. Sylvia Capp, 53 years old, has a physical examination, and it is determined that she is hypertensive. She attends the medical clinic and is receiving health instruction and supervision. Ms. Capp is to receive a thiazide drug and a diet low in fat, sodium, and triglycerides.

11. The finding that would constitute a significant index of hypertension is a 11.____

A. pulse deficit of 10 beats per minute
B. regular pulse of 90 beats per minute
C. systolic pressure fluctuating between 150 and 160 mm. Hg.
D. sustained diastolic pressure greater than 90 mm. Hg.

12. The nurse asks Ms. Capp to select foods that best meet her diet prescription. 12.____
Ms. Capp's knowledge of goods lowest in both fat and sodium would be ACCURATE if she selected

A. tossed salad with blue cheese dressing, cold cuts, and vanilla cookies
B. split pea soup, cheese sandwich, and a banana
C. cold baked chicken, lettuce with sliced tomatoes, and applesauce
D. beans and frankfurters, carrot and celery sticks, and a plain cupcake

13. When teaching Ms. Capp about her diet, the nurse should include which of these instructions? 13.____

A. Avoid eating canned fruits
B. Season your meat with lemon juice or vinegar
C. Restrict your intake of green vegetables
D. Drink diet soda instead of decaffeinated coffee

14. To assist Ms. Capp to comply with a low-fat diet, the information about fats that would be MOST useful to her is the 14.____

A. amount of fat in processed meats
B. method of preparing foods to limit the fat content
C. comparison of hydrogenated fats to emulsified fats
D. caloric differences of foods containing fats and carbohydrates

15. Because Ms. Capp is receiving a thiazide drug, her diet should include foods that are high in 15.____

A. calcium
B. potassium
C. iron
D. magnesium

16. Ms. Capp tells the nurse that she smokes two packs of cigarettes a day. 16.____
To initiate a plan that will assist Ms. Capp in overcoming her smoking habit, which of these actions by the nurse would probably be MOST effective?

A. Have her identify those times when she feels that she must have a cigarette
B. Ask her to describe what she knows about the deleterious effects of smoking on her condition
C. Explain to her how smoking contributes to environmental pollution
D. Impress on her the realization that smoking is a form of addiction that is no longer socially acceptable

Questions 17-25.

DIRECTIONS: Questions 17 through 25 are to be answered on the basis of the following information.

Mr. Ethan Allen, 46 years old, is admitted to a center for the treatment of persons who abuse alcohol. He had been drinking a quart or more of liquor a day for 10 to 15 years. He was drinking up to the time of his admission. His wife is with him.

17. Mr. Allen's immediate treatment is MOST likely to include orders for 17.____

A. oral fluids, ascorbic acid, and a narcotic
B. a cool bath, a barbiturate, and blood lithium level
C. full diet as tolerated, thiamine, and a tranquilizer
D. a spinal tap, bromides, and restraints

18. If Mr. Allen develops delirium tremens, which of these environmental factors is likely to be MOST disturbing? 18.____

A. Strangers
B. Shadows
C. Unfamiliar procedures
D. Medicinal odors

19. Ms. Allen says to the nurse, *I'd do anything to help my husband stop drinking.* 19.____
The PRIMARY goal of the nurse's response should be to

A. get Ms. Allen to clarify the problem as she sees it
B. have Ms. Allen join Al-Anon
C. tell Ms. Allen that she has done all she could to help her husband
D. have Ms. Allen understand that alcoholism is a problem that only her husband can solve

20. In giving care to Mr. Allen, the nurse should be alert for complications of withdrawal, which include 20.____

A. aphasia
B. hypotension
C. diarrhea
D. convulsions

21. After several weeks of group therapy, Mr. Allen says to the nurse, *I've never been able to face life without alcohol.* 21.____
Which of the responses would initially be MOST appropriate?

A. I know how you feel, Mr. Allen. We all have difficulty in meeting some problems.
B. But now you know where to go for help.
C. Perhaps you can manage if you join Alcoholics Anonymous, Mr. Allen.
D. That has been the way you have dealt with your problems.

22. Mr. Allen's success in abstaining from drinking is thought to depend on his 22.____

A. admission that his behavior is detrimental to himself and his family
B. conviction that he must change and has some capacity for change
C. ability to express remorse
D. having taken a pledge witnessed by fellow alcoholics

23. Mr. Allen is started on disulfiram (Antabuse), which he will continue to take after discharge from the hospital. It should be emphasized to Mr. Allen that while he is on Antabuse, he must NEVER take 23.____

    A. elixir of terpin hydrate
    B. aspirin
    C. bicarbonate of soda
    D. antihistamines

24. Patients such as Mr. Allen may develop Korsakoff's psychosis. Which of these symptoms is associated with this condition? 24.____

    A. Fantastic delusions and fear
    B. Sullenness and suspiciousness
    C. Amnesia and confabulation
    D. Nihilistic ideas and tearfulness

25. The nurse explains Alcoholics Anonymous to Mr. Allen. An understanding implemented by Alcoholics Anonymous is that people 25.____

    A. feel less alone when they feel understood
    B. are more likely to be able to handle problems when they are alerted to them ahead of time
    C. are dependent upon their environment for cues that keep them oriented
    D. resort to defense mechanisms as a means of coping with anxiety

---

KEY (CORRECT ANSWERS}

1. A
2. D
3. C
4. B
5. B
6. A
7. B
8. B
9. D
10. B
11. D
12. C
13. B
14. B
15. B
16. A
17. C
18. B
19. A
20. D
21. D
22. B
23. A
24. C
25. A

EXAMINATION SECTION
TEST 1

DIRECTIONS: Each question or incomplete statement is followed by several suggested answers or completions. Select the one that BEST answers the question or completes the statement. *PRINT THE LETTER OF THE CORRECT ANSWER IN THE SPACE AT THE RIGHT.*

1. The purpose of treating Parkinson's disease with Levodopa is to 1.____

   A. increase the production of acetylcholine
   B. replace dopamine in the brain cells
   C. improve the myelination of the neurons of the basal ganglia
   D. regenerate the neurons of the basal ganglia

2. Which of the following is NOT a possible major side effect of tetracyclines? 2.____

   A. Impaired kidney function
   B. Bone defects (in small children)
   C. Phototoxicity
   D. Neurotoxicity

3. Which of the following drugs may be prescribed for the prevention and treatment of gout? 3.____

   A. Acetominophen
   B. Hydrocortisone
   C. Colchicine
   D. Ibuprofen

4. A client with tetanus should be observed closely for 4.____

   A. pallor and perspiration
   B. respiratory spasms
   C. muscled rigidity
   D. involuntary muscle spasms

5. Vomiting should NOT be induced for poisonings involving 5.____

   A. acetaminophen
   B. petroleum distillates
   C. plant parts
   D. salicylate

6. After a spinal cord injury, a client should be encouated to drink fluids in order to 6.____

   A. prevent meningal infections
   B. avoid gangrene
   C. prevent urinary tract infections
   D. balance fluids and electrolytes

7. A nurse should use a tilt table in treating an arthritic client in order to 7.____

   A. prevent pressure ulcers
   B. prevent calcium loss
   C. promote spinal hyperextension
   D. prevent muscular atrophy

8. For an unimmunized 14-month-old, initial immunizations would include each of the following EXCEPT 8.____

   A. oral poliovirus vaccine
   B. DTP
   C. Td
   D. tuberculin test

9. Which lobe of the cerebral cortex is responsible for registering general sensations of heat, cold, pain, and touch? 9.____

   A. Occipital
   B. Parietal
   C. Temporal
   D. Frontal

10. A client is admitted to the emergency room with a sucking stab wound on the right side of the thorax. Into what position should the nurse place the client? 10.____

    A. On the back, with the head elevated
    B. In a high-Fowler's position with the right side supported
    C. On the left side, flat, with a pillow supporting the left arm
    D. On the right side, with the head elevated

11. The FIRST symptom of open-angle glaucoma is 11.____

    A. persistent headaches
    B. continually blurred vision
    C. uncontrollable twitching of the eye
    D. impaired peripheral vision

12. Respiratory isolation would be recommended for a client with 12.____

    A. cholera
    B. diphtheria
    C. laryngeal tuberculosis
    D. meningitis

13. The diet for a client being treated for ulcerative colitis may include each of the following EXCEPT 13.____

    A. raw bran
    B. milk
    C. hot cereal
    D. sliced apple

14. Which of the following is a common early symptom of myasthenia gravis? 14.____

    A. Blurred vision
    B. Double vision
    C. Migraine headaches
    D. Tearing

15. A client taking ampicillin at home should notify the physician 15.____

    A. if diarrhea develops
    B. when symptoms disappear entirely
    C. when a negative culture is obtained
    D. if drowsiness occurs

16. If a client experiences a generalized motor seizure, the nurse's primary responsibility is to 16.____

    A. insert a plastic airway between the teeth
    B. restrain the client's movements for safety
    C. clear the immediate environment for safety
    D. administer the prescribed anticonvulsant

17. For what purpose are clients encouraged to perform deep breathing exercises following surgery? 17.____

A. Increasing cardiac output
B. Expanding residual volume
C. Increasing blood volume
D. Counteracting respiratory acidosis

18. Which of the following would be experienced by a client with multiple sclerosis? 18.____

A. Tremors
B. Double vision
C. Mental confusion
D. Respiratory congestion

19. To reduce the risk of toxoplasmosis, pregnant women should be taught to avoid 19.____

A. cleaning the cat box
B. unprotected sex
C. stagnant pools of water
D. eating marine animals

20. For a client who has just undergone an above-the-knee amputation, the nurse should work to avoid a hip contracture by 20.____

A. making sure the client lies in the prone position several times a day
B. making sure the client sits in a chair frequently throughout the day
C. propping the stump with pillows
D. elevating the head of the client's bed

21. Following the repair of an inguinal hernia, the nurse can BEST help the recovering client by 21.____

A. applying an abdominal binder
B. encouraging frequent coughing
C. placing a rolled towel under the scrotum
D. encouraging a high-carbohydrate diet

22. Which of the following would MOST likely be discovered during a nursing assessment of a client with Meniere's disease? 22.____

A. Hypotension
B. Diplopia
C. Hearing loss
D. Jerky lateral eye movement

23. Due to concern for the development of blackwater fever, a client with malaria should be closely observed for 23.____

A. dark red urine
B. low-grade fever
C. vomiting
D. nausea

24. Which of the following substances is released by axons supplying skeletal muscles? 24.____

A. Potassium
B. Acetylcholine
C. ATP
D. Epinephrine

25. Which of the following is NOT considered to be an antimicrobial secretion of the human body? 25.____

A. Tears
B. Gastric juice
C. Mucus
D. Vaginal secretions

KEY (CORRECT ANSWERS)

1. B
2. D
3. B
4. B
5. B

6. C
7. B
8. C
9. C
10. D

11. D
12. D
13. B
14. B
15. A

16. C
17. D
18. B
19. A
20. A

21. C
22. D
23. A
24. B
25. C

TEST 2

DIRECTIONS: Each question or incomplete statement is followed by several suggested answers or completions. Select the one that BEST answers the question or completes the statement. *PRINT THE LETTER OF THE CORRECT ANSWER IN THE SPACE AT THE RIGHT.*

1. Which of the following is the MOST likely cause of osteoporosis? 1.____

   A. Iron deficiency
   B. Prolonged inactivity
   C. Prolonged period of low WBC
   D. Estrogen therapy

2. Which of the following is an early sign of lead poisoning in children? 2.____

   A. Mental confusion
   B. Anemia
   C. Tremors
   D. Yellow sclerae

3. If a client's mouth appears pulled to the right, it is an indication of injury to the _______ nerve. 3.____

   A. left vestibular
   B. left trigeminal
   C. right abducent
   D. right facial

4. Which of the following medications would NOT be used to treat gangrene? 4.____

   A. Tetracycline
   B. Chloramphenicol
   C. Streptomycin sulfate
   D. Penicillin G

5. Which of the following would be experienced by a client with tic doulourex, or trigeminal neuralgia? 5.____

   A. Yellow sclerae
   B. Uncontrollable twitching of eyelid
   C. Unilateral muscle paralysis
   D. Extreme head and facial pain

6. Following a laminectomy, which of the following is the primary postoperative complication that should be observed for? 6.____

   A. Cerebral edema
   B. Compression of spinal cord
   C. Bladder spasms
   D. Increased intracranial pressure

7. Each of the following results from a streptococci infection that enters via the upper respiratory tract EXCEPT 7.____

   A. mononucleosis
   B. puerperal sepsis
   C. rheumatic fever
   D. shigellosis

8. After being admitted to the emergency room for injuries sustained in a serious automobile accident, a client undergoes a splenectomy. In the immediate postoperative period, the nurse should watch for 8.____

A. intestinal bleeding or obstruction
B. peritonitis
C. hemorrhage or distended abdomen
D. infection or shock

9. What type of stool should be expected from a client that has a colostomy on the left side of the abdomen? 9.____

A. Coated with stringy mucus
B. Bloody
C. Moist and formed
D. Liquid

10. In bites involving the lower extremities, the incubation period for rabies is about 10.____

A. 10 days B. 40 days C. 2 months D. 4 months

11. Clients with spinal cord injuries sometimes experience sympathetic hyperreflexia. Each of the following is a sign or symptom of this condition EXCEPT 11.____

A. pulsating headache
B. goose bumps
C. pallor
D. diaphoresis

12. Which of the following positions would be appropriate for a client suffering from cerebral thrombosis? 12.____

A. Semi-Fowler's
B. Sims'
C. Trendlenburg
D. Prone

13. A diagnosis of *thrush* actually refers to a(n) 13.____

A. acid-fast bacterial infection
B. protozoan parasite
C. virus
D. yeast infection

14. Osteoarthritis is MOST likely to involve the joints of the 14.____

A. metacarpals and fingers
B. knees and hips
C. shoulders and elbows
D. metatarsals and ankles

15. Which of the following laboratory tests would be helpful in confirming a diagnosis of systemic lupus erythematosus? 15.____

A. WBC
B. Blood pH
C. Blood gases
D. BUN

16. Which of the following is NOT a therapeutic intervention involved in the treatment of tetanus? 16.____

A. Penicillin G
B. Diazepam to limit spasms
C. Cleansing of would with aqueous benzalkonium chloride
D. Wound debridement to allow exposure to air

17. A client experiencing left hemiplagia following a cerebral vascular accident would suffer paralysis of each of the following EXCEPT the 17.____

A. left arm
B. left eyelid
C. left leg
D. right side of the face

18. Which of the following, observed in a client, would indicate malaria? 18.____

A. Erythrocytosis
B. Leukocytosis
C. Splenomegaly
D. Increased sedimentation rate

19. Which of the following side effects may be a consequence of treating cerebral edema with dexamethasone? 19.____

A. Involuntary muscle contracture
B. Hypotension
C. Increased intracranial pressure
D. Hyperglycemia

20. *Full-thickness* burns are so classified because they have extended to involve damage to the 20.____

A. epidermis
B. upper dermis
C. subcutaneous layer
D. muscular tissue

21. The MAJOR problem encountered by newly paraplegic clients is 21.____

A. atrophy
B. control of the bladder
C. ambulation
D. formation of urinary calculi

22. When the spinal cord is crushed above the level of the phrenic nerve origin, _______ will result. 22.____

A. respiratory paralysis
B. vagus nerve dysfunction
C. cardiac arrhythmia
D. retention of sensation in lower extremities

23. An adolescent epileptic client who has been taking Dilantin develops status epilepticus. The MOST likely reason for this is that the 23.____

A. prescribed dosage of Dilantin was insufficient for the client's activity level
B. client failed to take the prescribed dosage consistently
C. client has built up a tolerance for the prescribed dosage
D. seizures are becoming more intense in response to the prescribed dosage

24. The test that is performed immediately to confirm a diagnosis of meningitis is 24.____

A. blood culture
B. lumbar puncture
C. meningomyelogram
D. alkaline phosphatase

25. Which of the following is the relay center for sensory impulses? 25.____

A. Thalamus
B. Cerebellum
C. Medulla oblongata
D. Pons

KEY (CORRECT ANSWERS)

1. B
2. B
3. D
4. C
5. D

6. B
7. D
8. C
9. C
10. D

11. C
12. B
13. D
14. B
15. D

16. C
17. B
18. C
19. D
20. C

21. B
22. A
23. B
24. B
25. A

TEST 3

DIRECTIONS: Each question or incomplete statement is followed by several suggested answers or completions. Select the one that BEST answers the question or completes the statement. *PRINT THE LETTER OF THE CORRECT ANSWER IN THE SPACE AT THE RIGHT.*

1. What type of antibiotics operate by blocking tRNA attachment to cell ribosomes? 1.____

   A. Tetracyclines
   B. Erythromycins
   C. Cephalosporins
   D. Penicillins

2. The primary goal of the medical treatment of chronic glaucoma is 2.____

   A. preventing secondary infections
   B. pupil dilation
   C. increasing ocular range of motion
   D. the control of intraocular pressure

3. A client with a peptic ulcer would be permitted to eat or drink each of the following EXCEPT 3.____

   A. milk
   B. oatmeal
   C. applesauce
   D. orange juice

4. After a fracture of the hip, what is/are the MOST frequently developed contracture(s)? 4.____

   A. Flexion and adduction of the hip
   B. Hyperextension of the knee
   C. External rotation
   D. Internal rotation

5. Which of the following clinical findings would NOT support a diagnosis of Crohn's disease? 5.____

   A. Occult blood in stool
   B. Anemia
   C. Elevated WBC
   D. Severe pain in right lower quadrant

6. Which of the following produce antibodies? 6.____

   A. Erythrocytes
   B. Plasma cells
   C. Eosiniphils
   D. Lymphocytes

7. Which of the following is NOT a common cause of gastritis? 7.____

   A. Chronic uremia
   B. Allergic reactions
   C. Zollinger-Ellison syndrome
   D. Bacterial or viral infection

8. When administering chloramphenicol to an infected client, a nurse should 8.____

   A. observe for anticoagulant effect
   B. observe for neuromuscular blockage

C. assess blood work before and during therapy
D. be watchful for false positive urine tests

9. A client with rheumatoid arthritis should be taught to 9.____

A. maintain the limbs in a position of extension
B. place pillows beneath the knees
C. remain in a semi-Fowler's position as long as possible
D. assume positions that are most comfortable

10. A client, who was earlier admitted with multiple serious injuries sustained in an accident, is diagnosed with a stress ulcer. The nurse should watch for, and immediately report, 10.____

A. nausea and headache
B. diaphoresis and cold extremities
C. diarrhea and distention
D. warm, flushed skin and complaints of thirst

11. Because of the behavior of damaged cells, clients with serious burns should have levels of _______ checked frequently. 11.____

A. vitamin A
B. sodium
C. potassium
D. calcium

12. Injury or infection of the _______ nerve is MOST likely to be the cause of nerve deafness. 12.____

A. facial
B. trigeminal
C. cochlear
D. vestibular

13. Each of the following is a symptom of severe cinchonism EXCEPT 13.____

A. deafness
B. blood in the urine
C. severe nausea
D. vertigo

14. The irreversible effects of untreated lead poisoning are imposed mainly upon the _______ system. 14.____

A. lymphatic
B. digestive
C. urinary
D. central nervous

15. Which of the following signs would indicate developing thrombophlebitis following pelvic surgery? 15.____

A. Edematous ankles
B. A painful, tender area on the leg
C. A reddened area at ankle and knee joints
D. Pruritis on the thigh

16. Which of the following would increase a client's risk of osteoporosis? 16.____

A. A history of hyperparathyroidism
B. Long-term steroid therapy
C. Excessive estrogen consumption
D. Frequent strenuous physical activity

17. What is the term for an internal antimicrobial protein agent that destroys certain gram-negative bacteria and viruses? 17.____

A. Properdin
B. Lysozyme
C. Amantadine
D. Interferon

18. Nerve fibers that are destroyed in the brain or spinal cord do not regenerate because they do not have 18.____

A. nuclei
B. a sodium pump
C. a neurilemma
D. a myelin sheath

19. Which crutch gait should be taught to a client fitted with a prosthesis after a single leg amputation? 19.____

A. Three-point
B. Four-point
C. Swing-through
D. Tripod

20. After surgery of the biliary tract, clients are at risk for developing respiratory infections because 20.____

A. bile in the blood causes lowered resistance
B. pathogens are transferred from bile to the blood
C. the incision is adjacent to the diaphragm
D. the anesthesia involved in lengthy surgery weakens immunity

21. When assessing a client suspected for increased intra-cranial pressure, the nurse may expect to discover any of the following EXCEPT 21.____

A. rapid pulse rate
B. psychotic behavior
C. nausea or vomiting
D. impaired pupil reactivity

22. When an organism enters a wound and produces a toxin which causes crepitus, what disease has been produced? 22.____

A. Salmonella
B. Botulism
C. Gas gangrene
D. Tetanus

23. Which of the following laboratory tests should a nurse refer to in order to aid in the diagnosis of arthritis? 23.____

A. Creatinine level
B. Bence Jones protein
C. Antinuclear antibody
D. Sodium level

24. Which of the following is a characteristic manifestation of rabies? 24.____

A. Confusion or memory loss
B. Pharyngeal spasm
C. Echolalia
D. Diarrhea

25. Which of the following assessment findings would NOT support a diagnosis of hiatal hernia? 25.____

A. Nocturnal dyspnea
B. Regurgitation
C. Respiratory pain
D. Heartburn after eating

KEY (CORRECT ANSWERS)

1. A
2. D
3. D
4. A
5. A
6. B
7. C
8. C
9. A
10. D
11. C
12. C
13. B
14. D
15. B
16. B
17. A
18. C
19. B
20. C
21. A
22. C
23. C
24. B
25. C

TEST 4

DIRECTIONS: Each question or incomplete statement is followed by several suggested answers or completions. Select the one that BEST answers the question or completes the statement. *PRINT THE LETTER OF THE CORRECT ANSWER IN THE SPACE AT THE RIGHT.*

1. Which of the following is considered to be the MOST common complication of peptic ulcer? 1.____

   A. Varices of the esophagus
   B. Perforation
   C. Hemorrhage
   D. Pyloric stenosis

2. A client is admitted to the emergency room following a serious automobile accident in which she suffered head injuries. Soon after admission, her temperature is measured at 102.6°F. 2.____
   This suggests an injury to the

   A. pons Varolii
   B. optic chiasm
   C. temporal lobe
   D. hypothalamus

3. Which of the following side effects may be experienced by a client taking sulfonamides for treatment of a urinary tract infection? 3.____

   A. Diarrhea
   B. Fatigue
   C. Photosensitivity
   D. Nephrotoxicity

4. A client suffering from myasthenia gravis would receive a dosage of neostigmine in order to 4.____

   A. accelerate neural transmission
   B. block the action of cholinesterase
   C. stimulate the cerebral cortex
   D. boost immunity

5. When tetracycline is given orally, it should be given 5.____

   A. an hour before milk or dairy products are ingested
   B. with a meal or snack
   C. with an antacid
   D. with orange juice or other citrus juice

6. 48 hours after a cerebral vascular accident, the client should begin 6.____

   A. exercises designed to actively return muscle function
   B. isometric exercises
   C. active exercises of all extremities
   D. passive range-of-motion exercises

7. Following surgery, a client's feedings are administered by nasogastric tube. Shortly after the feedings begin, the client develops diarrhea. 7.____
   Which of the following is a possible solution?

A. Decreasing the carbohydrate content of the formula
B. Decreasing the protein content of the formula
C. Diluting the formula with water
D. Switching to IV feedings

8. Which of the following is a common side effect associated with Dilantin? 8.____

A. Facial tics
B. Impaired pupil response
C. Tinnitus
D. Hypertrophy of the gums

9. Contact isolation would be imposed on a client with each of the following infections EXCEPT 9.____

A. impetigo
B. chickenpox
C. herpes simplex
D. acute respiratory infections in children

10. A client with an ileostomy would normally present a stool that is 10.____

A. solid and clay-colored
B. flecked with blood
C. liquid
D. pencil-shaped

11. When caring for a child with acute laryngitis, the nurse's main concern should be 11.____

A. reduction of fever
B. constant delivery of 40% humidified oxygen
C. increased fluid intake
D. constant respiratory monitoring

12. Which of the following medications is used to treat tic doulourex, or trigeminal neuralgia? 12.____

A. Morphine sulfate
B. Carbamazepine
C. Halol
D. Allopurinol

13. A client who suffered a spinal cord injury three weeks earlier suffers from coffee-ground emesis and restlessness. The nurse should 13.____

A. check hemoglobin levels in laboratory reports
B. insert a nasogastric tube
C. change the client to a liquid diet
D. check for occult blood in the stool

14. Following a splenectomy, a client should be observed carefully for the depletion of 14.____

A. vitamin A
B. potassium
C. calcium
D. sodium

15. A nurse could expect each of the following clinical findings from a client with Lyme disease EXCEPT 15.____

A. swollen joints
B. enlarged spleen
C. lack of coordination
D. paralysis

16. By what route do meningitis-producing bacteria enter the central nervous system? 16.____

A. Sinuses
B. Pores
C. Gastrointestinal tract
D. Urinary tract

17. Which of the following results from a Group A beta-hemolytic streptococcal infection? 17.____

A. Mononucleosis
B. Rheumatic fever
C. Rheumatoid arthritis
D. Hepatitis A

18. Which of the following drugs is MOST commonly used to treat rheumatoid arthritis? 18.____

A. Gold salts
B. Hydrocortisone
C. Aspirin
D. Ibuprofen

19. Worsening colitis is often treated by placing the patient on a bland, residue-free diet and by administering vitamins parenterally. The purpose of this treatment is to 19.____

A. increase intestinal absorption
B. reduce gastric acidity
C. minimize colonic irritation
D. boost electrolytes

20. Stump shrinkage following an amputation is caused by muscular atrophy and 20.____

A. subcutaneous fat reduction
B. postoperative edema
C. loss of bone tissue
D. skin turgor

21. During a client's early post-burn phase, the nurse's PRIMARY objective should be to 21.____

A. restore fluid volume
B. initiate tissue repair
C. relieve pain
D. prevent infection

22. Which of the following would NOT typically be part of a nursing care plan for a client with systemic lupus erythematosus? 22.____

A. Dosages of vitamin C
B. Renal dialysis
C. Administration of corticosteroids
D. Avoiding exposure to sunlight

23. Which of the following is a serious complication of acute malaria? 23.____

A. Fluid and electrolyte imbalance
B. Lung congestion
C. Seizure of peristalsis
D. Anemia

24. Gold salts used to treat rhematoid arthritis involve the serious side effect of 24.____

A. emboli
B. gastric pain
C. decreased cardiac output
D. kidney damage

25. Which of the following is NOT a gram-negative, rod-shaped bacteria? 25.____

A. Shigella
B. Neisseria
C. Escherichia
D. Salmonella

KEY (CORRECT ANSWERS)

1. C
2. D
3. C
4. B
5. A

6. D
7. A
8. D
9. B
10. C

11. D
12. B
13. A
14. B
15. B

16. A
17. B
18. C
19. C
20. A

21. A
22. B
23. A
24. D
25. B

EXAMINATION SECTION
TEST 1

DIRECTIONS: Each question or incomplete statement is followed by several suggested answers or completions. Select the one that BEST answers the question or completes the statement. *PRINT THE LETTER OF THE CORRECT ANSWER IN THE SPACE AT THE RIGHT.*

1. Each of the following is a therapeutic intervention involved in treating a client who has suffered carbon monoxide poisoning EXCEPT 1.____

   A. administering 50% glucose or mannitol
   B. administering 60% oxygen until respirations are normal
   C. artificial respiration
   D. administering synthetic erythrocytes (Flousol) which will deliver oxygen to cells in the presence of CO

2. The average adult woman should undergo Pap smear screening 2.____

   A. every three years until age 40, and annually after that
   B. every three years following 3 initial negative annual tests
   C. annually if sexually active; every three years if abstinent
   D. annually after the age of 18

3. Which of the following types of joints is LEAST likely to be affected by osteoarthritis? 3.____

   A. Shoulder B. Knee C. Finger D. Hip

4. The symptoms of left-sided congestive heart failure would be most evident in the 4.____

   A. hepatic system
   B. systemic circulation
   C. pulmonary system
   D. organs

5. When interviewing a client diagnosed with laryngeal cancer, a nurse would be most likely to learn of a history of 5.____

   A. smoking
   B. high-fat, low-fiber diet
   C. poverty
   D. heavy alcohol use

6. Dorothea Orem's systems model of nursing involves each of the following systems EXCEPT 6.____

   A. wholly compensatory
   B. partly compensatory
   C. cognitive-affective
   D. supportive-educative

7. A client is admitted with a diagnosis of abdominal aortic aneurysm. Which of the following would the nurse expect to find when examining the client's abdomen? 7.____

   A. A small knotty protrusion
   B. Minimal bowel sounds
   C. A large throbbing mass
   D. A distended, rigid abdominal wall

8. A client with bacterial pneumonia appears slightly cyanotic on admission. The cyanosis is most likely the result of 8.____

A. poor circulation
B. low cardiac output
C. poor oxygenation of blood
D. iron-deficiency anemia

9. Which of the following would NOT typically be found in a patient with Addison's disease? 9.____

A. Edema
B. Hypoglycemia
C. Nausea
D. Hypotension

10. Which of the following actions should be involved in a home care plan for promoting joint movement for a child with juvenile rheumatoid arthritis? 10.____

A. Restricting daily dietary intake of purine
B. Applying cool compresses to affected joints
C. Cyclical weight-bearing exercises involving the affected joints
D. Applying moist heat to the affected joints

11. Drugs such as sulfasuxidine are used to prepare the cancerous bowel for surgery primarily for the purpose of 11.____

A. reducing colonic bacteria
B. reducing inflammation of tumors
C. maintaining electrolyte balance
D. ceasing peristalsis in the colon

12. Digoxin would be administered to a client in order to 12.____

A. strengthen the heartbeat
B. lower the blood pressure
C. dilate the blood vessels
D. even out heart rhythms

13. Which of the following would NOT typically be an element of a nursing care plan for a client with a pneumothorax? 13.____

A. Positioning in Trendlenburg position
B. Offering fluids frequently
C. Maintaining constant supervision until stable
D. Monitoring respiratory status

14. Following a subtotal thyroidectomy, a client is at risk for hypothyroidism. Which of the following is a typical symptom of this condition? 14.____

A. Fatigue
B. Joint pain
C. Translucent skin
D. Yellow sclerae

15. Which of the following would be the best position for a client diagnosed with a closed head injury? 15.____

A. Prone, with the head turned to the right
B. Prone, with head protruding slightly over the end of the bed and arms at the sides
C. Supine, with the head elevated 30°
D. Flat on the left side

16. What is the PRIMARY symptom of pituitary adenoma? 16.____

A. Visual defects
B. Fatigue and severe lethargy
C. Memory loss
D. Impotence

17. After a client undergoes a bronchoscopy, the nurse should 17.____

A. force fluids immediately
B. encourage the client to cough every two hours
C. encourage deep breathing
D. position the client in a side-lying position

18. Which of the following is a significant risk factor for myocardial infarction? 18.____

A. Hypotension
B. Atherosclerosis
C. Advanced age
D. Vigorous exercise

19. A client's blood gas tests, drawn while the client is breathing room air, show a $PaCO_2$ result of 78 mmHg. The conclusion that can be drawn from this is that the client is 19.____

A. hypoventilating
B. using oxygen therapy
C. acidotic
D. alkalotic

20. A client is diagnosed with a stage III carcinoma of the floor of the mouth. Following radiation therapy, the client should anticipate each of the following side effects EXCEPT 20.____

A. nausea
B. altered taste sensation
C. difficulty swallowing
D. inflamed mucosa

21. On the day following a bilateral adrenalectomy, a client's temperature is slightly elevated. The most likely cause of this is 21.____

A. dehydration
B. UTI
C. poor lung elasticity
D. infection

22. When interviewing a patient diagnosed with acute bacterial endocarditis, it is important to obtain information relating to 22.____

A. possible chemical exposure
B. recent infections
C. chest pain that has been relieved by rest
D. chronic pulmonary disease

23. An adolescent client admitted to the pediatric unit with asthma is given a theophylline infusion. Which of the following is NOT a typical sign of theophylline toxicity that a nurse should observe for? 23.____

A. Urinary retention
B. Nausea
C. Tachycardia
D. Vomiting

24. Testicular cancer is known to be associated with a history of 24.____

A. vasectomy
B. epididymitis

C. undescended testes
D. early onset of sexual relations

25. Each of the following is a symptom consistent with the diagnosis of ketoacidosis EXCEPT 25.____

A. glycosuria
B. decreased blood pH
C. decreased respiratory rate
D. polydipsia

KEY (CORRECT ANSWERS)

1. B
2. B
3. A
4. C
5. D

6. C
7. C
8. C
9. A
10. D

11. A
12. A
13. A
14. A
15. C

16. D
17. D
18. B
19. A
20. A

21. C
22. B
23. A
24. C
25. C

TEST 2

DIRECTIONS: Each question or incomplete statement is followed by several suggested answers or completions. Select the one that BEST answers the question or completes the statement. *PRINT THE LETTER OF THE CORRECT ANSWER IN THE SPACE AT THE RIGHT.*

1. Which of the following is considered to be a classic sign of lung cancer? 1.____

   A. Fever
   B. Bloody sputum
   C. Cough
   D. Constricted airway

2. Which of the following would be most likely to be an indication that a client is experiencing hypoxia? 2.____

   A. Anxiety
   B. Lethargy
   C. Aggression
   D. Euphoria

3. A client with congestive heart failure has an apical pulse rate of 44, and shows a regular heart beat with no ectopic beats. Most likely, the client will be treated with 3.____

   A. Lidocaine
   B. defibrillation
   C. Digitalis
   D. Atropine

4. A client is admitted to the emergency room after being hit by a car. The client was unconscious at the scene of the accident. 4.____
   Upon the client's arrival, the nurse's FIRST priority should be to

   A. establish IV access
   B. assess vital signs
   C. establish ventilation
   D. check pupils

5. The nurse should instruct a client with a permanent colostomy to 5.____

   A. avoid sudden movements
   B. limit fluid intake
   C. regularly eat breads and hard cheeses
   D. avoid foods containing roughage

6. Postural drainage would be contraindicated in a 6.____

   A. client with increased intracranial pressure who has lowered breath sounds
   B. client with emphysema who has difficulty bringing up secretions
   C. patient with chronic bronchitis
   D. preoperative client with excessive secretions from smoking

7. The most significant dietary modification for clients with angina pectoris should be 7.____

   A. avoiding dairy products
   B. eating smaller portions at each meal
   C. reducing calcium intake
   D. eating potassium-rich foods

8. According to Virginia Henderson's nursing model, nursing focuses on the 8.____

   A. individual
   B. illness
   C. individual's environment
   D. caring relationship

9. A client has just undergone total pelvic exenteration for uterine cancer. In the recovery room, one of the nursing care priorities should be to assist adequate pulmonary function. In what position should the client be positioned? 9.____

A. High Fowler's
B. Supine, with legs elevated
C. Prone, with arms at the sides
D. Low Fowler's

10. A person who is prescribed cortisone for treatment of rheumatoid arthritis should be observed for signs of 10.____

A. inflammation
B. anorexia
C. weight gain
D. soreness

11. Which of the following blood laboratory results is a typical finding of a myocardial infarction? 11.____

A. Below-normal WBC count
B. Below-normal albumin
C. Elevated CPK value
D. Elevated PO_2

12. Each of the following is considered to be a risk factor for cervical cancer EXCEPT 12.____

A. family history of cervical cancer
B. teenage pregnancy
C. sexual experiences with multiple partners
D. history of sexually-transmitted disease

13. A patient taking glucocorticoids for the treatment of Addison's disease should be instructed to 13.____

A. take them before exercise periods
B. take them with meals or an antacid
C. avoid taking them before the main meal of the day
D. take them on an empty stomach

14. During postoperative care for a client who has just undergone a total knee replacement for treatment of rheumatoid arthritis, the nurse should usually position the client with a priority on 14.____

A. preventing flexion deformities of the joints
B. decreasing edema around the joints
C. maximum comfort
D. preventing venous stasis

15. A patient with bladder cancer has an ileal conduit created. When the patient's urinary output falls below _______ ml/hour, it is a sign that excessive stomal edema is probably occurring. 15.____

A. 10
B. 20
C. 30
D. 40

16. A client with chest trauma has been prescribed morphine sulfate. Which of the following clinical findings would suggest that the client is experiencing a side effect from the medication? 16.____

A. Decreased respiratory rate
B. Inhibited mucus secretion
C. Visual hallucinations
D. Hypertension

17. Most often, the tip of the catheter on a pacemaker is placed in the 17.____

A. left ventricle
B. right ventricle
C. left atrium
D. right atrium

18. A client suffering from hyperpituitarism is likely to experience increased secretion of each of the following EXCEPT 18.____

A. prolactin (PRL)
B. growth hormone (GH)
C. vasopressin (ADH)
D. corticotrophic hormone (ACTH)

19. Which of the following is a symptom of hyperthyroidism? 19.____

A. Decreased libido
B. Protruding eyeballs
C. Edematous skin
D. Enlargement of the gland

20. Which of the following would be the most effective method of delivering oxygen prescribed at four liters per minute? 20.____

A. Rebreathing mask
B. Face mask
C. Nasal cannula
D. Tent

21. When using rotating tourniquets, the longest period of time blood flow should be decreased in any one of the client's extremities is ______ minutes. 21.____

A. 10
B. 30
C. 45
D. 90

22. A client develops tetany following a subtotal thyroidectomy. Which medications will most likely be ordered by the physician? 22.____

A. Sodium pentothal
B. Phospholine iodide
C. Calcium gluconate
D. Potassium chloride

23. Which of the following elements, disclosed during the client's interview and health history, would be most significant in predisposing a person to diabetes mellitus? 23.____

A. Indo-European ancestry
B. Cigarette smoking
C. Obesity
D. Childlessness

24. A 45-year-old woman has just been diagnosed with tuberculosis. The member of her family who would be at the greatest risk for contracting tuberculosis is her 24.____

A. grade-school children
B. adolescent children
C. 50-year-old husband
D. 79-year-old mother

25. A client diagnosed with cervical cancer has a radium implant in place. Which of the following types of diet is standard nursing care for such a client? 25.____

A. Low-cholesterol
B. Low-residue
C. High-fiber
D. Clear liquid

KEY (CORRECT ANSWERS)

1. C
2. A
3. D
4. C
5. D

6. A
7. B
8. A
9. D
10. C

11. C
12. B
13. B
14. A
15. C

16. A
17. B
18. C
19. B
20. B

21. C
22. C
23. C
24. D
25. B

TEST 3

DIRECTIONS: Each question or incomplete statement is followed by several suggested answers or completions. Select the one that BEST answers the question or completes the statement. *PRINT THE LETTER OF THE CORRECT ANSWER IN THE SPACE AT THE RIGHT.*

1. A positive test for HIV means the client 1.____

   A. is immune to AIDS
   B. has antibodies to the AIDS virus
   C. will develop AIDS
   D. has AIDS

2. The rising wave produced by a positive lead of the EKG as the ventricles depolarize is called the _______ wave. 2.____

   A. P B. Q C. R D. S

3. A client with histoplasmosis will present symptoms that mimic 3.____

   A. asthma
   B. tuberculosis
   C. embolism
   D. emphysema

4. In a patient receiving radiation therapy to the breast, which of the following symptoms would be most likely to occur? 4.____

   A. Dizziness
   B. Diarrhea
   C. Skin reactions
   D. Anorexia

5. A client is brought to the emergency room about 30 minutes after being involved in a serious car accident. The nurse assesses the client for signs of increasing intracranial pressure. 5.____
   Which of the following signs would not be indicative of this?

   A. Rising body temperature
   B. Tachycardia
   C. Rising systolic blood pressure
   D. Unequal pupil dilation

6. During the preoperative period for a client about to undergo an adrenalectomy, it is most important for the nurse to insure 6.____

   A. adequate nutrition
   B. electrolyte balance
   C. high fluid intake
   D. complete rest

7. After undergoing a mitral valve replacement, a client experiences persistent bleeding from the surgical incision. The nurse will most likely administer 7.____

   A. Coumadin
   B. Lasix
   C. vitamin C
   D. protamine sulfate

8. A client is admitted to the emergency room with a diagnosis of suspected thoracic spinal cord injury. The nurse's first priority of care would be to 8.____

   A. maintain cardiorespiratory function
   B. balance fluid and electrolyte levels

C. establish IV access
D. orient the client to his/her surroundings

9. To determine the existence of colon cancer, the screening test most likely to be performed is one that tests the client's stool for the presence of 9.____

A. cancerous cells
B. occult blood
C. large numbers of dead bacteria
D. mucus

10. When caring for a client with chest tubes, a nurse should 10.____

A. pin tubing to the bed to prevent the tube from pulling apart
B. secure all connections with adhesive tape to prevent disconnection
C. irrigate the tube with normal saline to prevent clogging
D. keep bottles at chest level to promote drainage

11. A client with cancer of the colon has recently undergone an abdominoperineal resection with a permanent colostomy. On the 4th postoperative day, an irrigation is ordered for the client. What is the primary purpose of this first colostomy irrigation? 11.____

A. Stimulating peristalsis
B. Cleansing the colon
C. Checking for occult blood
D. Dilating the sphincter

12. A parent of an asthmatic child asks about measures that can be taken at home to decrease the frequency of the child's asthmatic episodes. Which of the following nurse's suggestions would be most appropriate? 12.____

A. Vacuuming and dusting the entire house frequently
B. Using aerosol spray disinfectants around the house
C. Having the child sleep with the bedroom window open
D. Covering the child's mattress with a leather pad

13. Which of the following is not considered to be a risk factor for the development of breast cancer? 13.____

A. Breastfeeding
B. Family history of breast cancer
C. Childlessness
D. Menopause after age 50

14. A client with chronic obstructive pulmonary disease has complained that dyspnea interferes with her eating. The nurse should instruct the client to 14.____

A. eat large frequent meals
B. use oxygen at mealtimes
C. avoid foods that produce gas
D. avoid between-meal snacks

15. In the immediate postoperative period following a total laryngectomy, the primary nursing care goal should be 15.____

A. establishing nonverbal communication
B. preventing hemorrhage
C. maintaining a patent airway
D. relieving pain

16. As part of the nursing care plan of a client with systemic lupus erythematosus, the importance of which of the following dietary components should be stressed? 16.____

A. Vitamin C
B. Iron
C. Calcium
D. Vitamin A

17. Following a left orchiectomy, a client with malignant seminoma undergoes external radiotherapy to the lower abdomen. Which of the following side effects should the client be told is most likely? 17.____

A. Diarrhea
B. Impotence
C. Nausea
D. Hair loss

18. Which of the following nursing practices would NOT typically be involved in the care of a patient with hyperparathyroidism? 18.____

A. Require complete bed rest
B. Encourage intake of cranberry juice
C. Monitor intake and output
D. Limit calcium intake

19. Each of the following is a common side effect of nitro-glycerin EXCEPT 19.____

A. headache
B. shortness of breath
C. hypotension
D. dizziness

20. A client with Addison's disease is being taught by a nurse how to handle stress. The client should be taught that since some stress is unavoidable, a dietary modification that might prove helpful is to ______ during times of stress. 20.____

A. increase potassium intake
B. avoid carbohydrates
C. increase sodium intake
D. avoid proteins

21. Following a lung lobectomy, a patient is fitted with chest tubes attached to water-seal drainage. After some time, the nurse observes that the fluid in the chest and drainage tubes has stopped fluctuating.
This means that the 21.____

A. end of the chest tube is in the pleural space
B. lung has collapsed
C. mediastinal space has decreased
D. lung has fully expanded

22. The general adaptation syndrome (GAS), described by Hans Selye as a universal human response to environmental stressors, develops in distinct stages, including each of the following EXCEPT 22.____

A. the alarm reaction
B. resistance
C. denial
D. exhaustion

23. Which of the following is a long-term result of untreated hypertension? 23.____

A. Stroke
B. Liver failure
C. Diabetes
D. Obesity

24. A client with glomerulonephritis is most likely to experience 24.____

A. polyuria
B. dysuria
C. oliguria
D. anuria

25. Each of the following would be an appropriate element of a nursing care plan for a client with acute bacterial endocarditis EXCEPT 25.____

A. bed rest
B. observing for signs of embolism
C. a soft, low-cholesterol diet
D. observing for signs of heart failure

KEY (CORRECT ANSWERS)

1. B
2. C
3. B
4. C
5. B

6. D
7. D
8. A
9. B
10. B

11. A
12. A
13. A
14. C
15. C

16. A
17. A
18. A
19. B
20. C

21. D
22. C
23. A
24. C
25. C

EXAMINATION SECTION
TEST 1

DIRECTIONS: Each question or incomplete statement is followed by several suggested answers or completions. Select the one that BEST answers the question or completes the statement. *PRINT THE LETTER OF THE CORRECT ANSWER IN THE SPACE AT THE RIGHT.*

1. Normal inspiration is an active process that uses the diaphragm and external intercostal muscles. 1.____
   Ineffective breathing patterns can be manifested by all of the following EXCEPT

   A. use of accessory muscles for respiration
   B. increased breath sounds in lung segments
   C. paradoxical respiratory movement
   D. restlessness, anxiety, and diaphoresis

2. Postural drainage is indicated for patients who have difficulty clearing secretions due to airway obstruction and/or excessive mucus production. 2.____
   Signs of airway obstruction include

   A. tachycardia
   B. increased breath sounds with no crackles or gurgles
   C. increased oxygen saturation
   D. decreased respiratory rate

3. Therapeutic percussion is typically provided while the patient is in various PD positions. 3.____
   Percussions and vibrations are CONTRAINDICATED in

   A. spinal anesthesia
   B. thoracic skin grafts
   C. subcutaneous emphysema
   D. all of the above

4. It may be inappropriate to simply administer oxygen without conducting a thorough patient assessment to determine the cause of the hypoxemic event. 4.____
   Oxygen therapy is commonly prescribed in the initial treatment of all of the following conditions EXCEPT

   A. acute myocardial infarction
   B. tuberculosis
   C. severe trauma
   D. immediately following surgery or extubation

5. Breathing oxygen concentrations greater than 50% for more than 24 hours can cause injury to the lung tissue or oxygen toxicity. 5.____
   Early signs of oxygen toxicity include

   I. dyspnea, cough, lethargy, and vomiting
   II. restlessness
   III. retrosternal chest pain
   IV. hemoptasis

   The CORRECT answer is:

   A. I, II, III
   B. I, II, IV
   C. I, III, IV
   D. II, IV

6. Some patients continue oxygen therapy following discharge. Indications for home oxygen therapy include all of the following EXCEPT 6.____

   A. pulmonary hypertension
   B. recurring congestive heart failure
   C. anemia
   D. sleep apnea syndrome

7. Oxygen will not explode, but will cause something on fire to burn much faster. Important precautionary measures to prevent fire include 7.____

   A. no smoking in any room where oxygen is being used
   B. keep equipment at least 10 feet away from any open flame
   C. do not use oily lotions, face creams, grease, or lip balms around oxygen equipment
   D. all of the above

8. A transtracheal oxygen catheter is a thin, teflon-coated tube that is surgically placed into the trachea. 8.____
   Complications of transtracheal oxygen therapy include all of the following EXCEPT

   A. inflammation
   B. thin secretions
   C. bleeding
   D. infection

9. A metered-dose inhaler is a pressurized canister which releases an aerosol containing the drug suspended in a fluorocarbon gas stream. 9.____
   The nurse should provide the patient with instructions to

   A. assemble the inhaler
   B. shake the inhaler to mix the medication and propellent
   C. remove the cap from the mouthpiece
   D. all of the above

10. Artificial airways are devices designed to maintain patent communication between the tracheobronchial tree and the air supply in the external environment. 10.____
    Indications for an endotracheal tube include all of the following EXCEPT

    A. temporary measures for airway obstruction
    B. mechanical ventilation
    C. protection of nasal mucosa
    D. management of secretions

11. The main indication for the insertion of a nasal airway is to protect the nasal mucosa from the trauma of frequent passage of suction catheters. 11.____
    A MAJOR disadvantage of nasal airway insertion is

    A. it does not prevent occlusion of upper airway by tongue
    B. potential inability to speak
    C. potential for aspiration
    D. potential for laryngeal damage

12. For long-term use, tracheostomy is preferred over endotracheal intubation. Advantages of tracheostomy tubes include all of the following EXCEPT 12.____

A. direct communication with trachea
B. longer tube length results in less airway resistance than with endotracheal tubes
C. easily tolerated by patients
D. avoidance of trauma to larynx

13. Complications of intubation can be mechanical or physiologic in nature. _______ is a physiologic, not a mechanical, complication. 13.____

A. Tube displacement
B. Obstruction
C. Aspiration
D. Loss of cuff seal

14. Nursing diagnoses for patients on mechanical ventilation include nursing diagnoses common to intubated patients, such as 14.____

A. inadequate gas exchange related to increased secretions, interstitial edema, and shunt
B. high risk for decreased cardiac output related to decreased venous return
C. anxiety related to mechanical ventilation and severity of illness
D. all of the above

15. Acute sinusitis commonly accompanies or follows an upper respiratory tract infection. Of the following, the LEAST commonly involved organism is 15.____

A. C. defficle
B. H. influenzae
C. S. pyogens
D. S. pneumoniae

16. Anaerobic pathogens are the most common infectious cause of chronic sinusitis. Non-infectious contributors to chronic sinusitis include all of the following EXCEPT 16.____

A. smoking
B. amphetamine abuse
C. habitual nasal sprays or inhalants
D. history of allergy

17. Rhinitis is commonly caused by viral infection, as in acute rhinitis, or the common cold, coryza. 17.____
Known organisms in acute viral rhinitis include

I. rhinovirus
II. influenza and para-influenza
III. infectious mononucleosis
IV. coxsackie virus

The CORRECT answer is:

A. I, II, III
B. II, III
C. I, II, IV
D. I, II, III, IV

18. Nursing interventions to educate patients with rhinitis in order to prevent further infection include all of the following EXCEPT 18.____

A. disposing of tissues properly
B. using cloth handkerchiefs
C. using good handwashing techniques
D. covering mouth and nose when coughing and sneezing

19. Nasal obstruction is commonly caused by displacement of the nasal septum from the midline position. 19.____
Common results of nasal deviation include

A. nasal obstruction
B. postnasal drip
C. epistaxis
D. all of the above

20. The priority of goals established for the patient with epistaxis will depend on the severity of the problem and the presence or absence of associated complications. APPROPRIATE goals for patients with epistaxis include 20.____

A. normal vital signs and level of consciousness
B. adequate caloric intake
C. pain relief
D. all of the above

21. Nursing interventions while taking care of a patient with epistaxis include all of the following EXCEPT 21.____

A. immediate assessment of vital signs
B. positioning of the patient with foot end of the bed elevated
C. pressure applied to the nose
D. coaching in mouth breathing

22. When evaluating the care of a patient with epistaxis, the nurse considers which of the following assessment parameters? 22.____

I. Respiratory accessory muscles should not be used.
II. Cyanosis and diaphoresis should be absent.
III. Mucus membrane should remain pink and moist.

The CORRECT answer is:

A. *I only* B. I, II C. I, II, III D. II, III

23. The priority of goals established for the patient with a nasal fracture will depend on the severity of the problem and the presence or absence of associated complications. Appropriate goals for a patient with this problem include all of the following EXCEPT 23.____

A. patent airway and normal blood gas levels
B. elevated body temperature
C. pain relief
D. verbalization of acceptance of temporary disfigurement

24. The most common form of laryngeal cancer is squamous cell carcinoma. 24.____
The one of the following which is NOT a risk factor for laryngeal squamous cell carcinoma is

A. cocaine abuse
B. prolonged use of tobacco and alcohol
C. exposure to radiation
D. voice abuse

25. The earliest symptom of laryngeal cancer is hoarseness, or voice change. 25.____
Later manifestations include all of the following EXCEPT

A. increasing dyspnea
B. hematemesis
C. dysphagia
D. hemoptysis

KEY (CORRECT ANSWERS)

1. B
2. A
3. D
4. B
5. A
6. C
7. D
8. B
9. D
10. C
11. A
12. B
13. C
14. D
15. A
16. B
17. C
18. B
19. D
20. D
21. B
22. C
23. B
24. A
25. B

TEST 2

DIRECTIONS: Each question or incomplete statement is followed by several suggested answers or completions. Select the one that BEST answers the question or completes the statement. *PRINT THE LETTER OF THE CORRECT ANSWER IN THE SPACE AT THE RIGHT.*

1. An important role of the nurse is to instruct and assist the patient in producing an effective cough. 1.____
Factors that influence the ability to cough include all of the following EXCEPT

   A. analgesia may be needed before cough exercise
   B. oral hydration using ice chips or sips of water can make coughing easier
   C. a lying down position is the most effective and comfortable position
   D. splinting a painful area during coughing with gentle hand pressure helps the patient cough

2. Chronic obstructive pulmonary disease (COPD) is a broad term used to describe conditions characterized by chronic obstruction to expiratory air flow. 2.____
Complications of COPD include all of the following EXCEPT

   A. acute respiratory failure
   B. tuberculosis
   C. cor pulmonale
   D. pneumothorax

3. The priority goals of nursing intervention for patients with acute exacerbation of COPD are the maintenance of adequate oxygenation, ventilation, and airway clearance. The patient should display 3.____

   A. clear breath sounds with no crackles
   B. respiratory rate between 12-20 breaths/minute at rest
   C. arterial PO_2 at patient's normal baseline
   D. all of the above

4. The etiological factors of asthma are not completely understood, but it is clear that asthma can develop after exposure to a variety of substances. 4.____
Asthma is characterized by all of the following EXCEPT

   A. hemoptosis
   B. reversible airway obstruction
   C. airway inflammation
   D. airway hyperresponsiveness

5. The severity of an asthma attack is reflected by the degree of airflow obstruction, level of oxygenation, and nature of breathing patterns. 5.____
Patients at increased risk for life-threatening asthma attacks do NOT include those

   A. less than 1 year old
   B. with PEFR or FEV_1 below 25% of predicted level
   C. with PCO_2 below 40 mmHg
   D. with wide daily fluctuation in PEFR or FEV_1

6. Which of the following is associated with an acute asthma attack? 6.____
   I. Impaired gas exchange related to ventilation-per-fusion mismatch, impaired diffusion, or arterio-venous shunting
   II. Fatigue related to increased efforts to breathe
   III. Fluid volume deficit related to increased intake and decreased insensible loss

   The CORRECT answer is:

   A. I *only*
   B. I, II
   C. I, II, III
   D. II, III

7. Outcome criteria for a patient with asthma include all of the following EXCEPT that the patient 7.____

   A. maintain $PaCO_2$ at approximately 40 mmHg
   B. have clear breath sounds on auscultation
   C. maintain PaO_2 at approximately 50 mmHg
   D. report no breathlessness at rest and minimal with activities

8. Restrictive lung diseases encompass a vast array of disorders that lead to decreased lung inflation. 8.____
   A hallmark of all restrictive disorders, regardless of cause, is

   A. decreased lung volume
   B. decreased breath sounds
   C. decreased vital capacity
   D. increased residual volume

9. Restrictive disorders are associated with 9.____

   A. ineffective breathing pattern related to increased lung inflation
   B. impaired gas exchange related to increased surface area for diffusion
   C. activity intolerance related to impaired gas exchange
   D. all of the above

10. Adult respiratory distress syndrome (ARDS) is a common problem, and 65% of cases are fatal. 10.____
    Major causes of ARDS include all of the following EXCEPT

    A. multiple sclerosis
    B. multiple blood transfusions
    C. aspiration of gastric contents
    D. trauma and sepsis

11. It has been reported that inspiratory pressures greater than 70 cm H_2O are associated with a 43% risk of barotrauma. 11.____
    Risk factors for barotrauma include

    A. low residual volume
    B. large tidal volume
    C. low levels of PEEP
    D. low peak airway pressure

12. Barotrauma is the presence of air outside the alveolus and is manifested by 12.____
    I. pulmonary interstitial emphysema
    II. pneumomediastinum
    III. tension lung cysts

    The CORRECT answer is:

    A. I, II
    B. II *only*
    C. I, III
    D. I, II, III

13. The aim of therapy in a patient of ARDS is to support lung function until healing occurs and to prevent the development of complications related to medical therapy and the underlying disease process. 13.____
    Goals of therapeutic management include

    A. optimizing gas exchange
    B. maintaining adequate tissue perfusion
    C. controlling the underlying problem that precipitated ARDS
    D. all of the above

14. Nursing care for the patient with ARDS is planned to maintain respiratory and hemodynamic stability. 14.____
    Outcome criteria for the patient include all of the following EXCEPT

    A. PaO_2 below 60 mmHg on 40% FIO_2 with a shunt fraction of less than 20%
    B. peak airway pressure below 40-50 mmHg
    C. skin remains intact
    D. stable weight

15. Generally, mechanical ventilation of COPD patients is avoided if at all possible. 15.____
    Mechanical ventilation is NOT deemed necessary when

    A. conservative therapy has failed to improve hypoxemia/acidosis or has resulted in progressive somnolence
    B. the patient is exhausted
    C. the patient has severe hyperoxemia and alkalosis and is unable to cooperate because of altered mental status
    D. the patient is unable to expectorate secretions

16. The nursing care for COPD patients in acute respiratory failure is planned to achieve which of the following outcomes? 16.____

    A. Breathing pattern and arterial blood gas levels return to prefailure levels
    B. Lungs clear to auscultation
    C. Airway remains patent
    D. All of the above

17. Pneumonia is an inflammation of the lower respiratory tract that involves the lung parenchyma, including alveoli and supportive structures. 17.____
    The organism MOST commonly involved in the causation of community acquired pneumonia is

    A. klebsiella pneumonia
    B. staphylococcus aureus
    C. streptococcus pnemoniae
    D. pseudomonas aeruginosa

18. Hospital acquired, or nosocomial, pneumonias are LEAST commonly caused by 18.____

A. pseudomonas aeruginosa
B. klebsiella pneumonia
C. streptococcus pneumoniae
D. staphylococcus aureus

19. Which of the following persons are at INCREASED risk for aspiration pneumonia? 19.____

I. Drug abusers
II. Impaired gag or swallowing reflex
III. Alcoholics

The CORRECT answer is:

A. I, II
B. I, II, III
C. I, III
D. II *only*

20. Viral pneumonia in immunosuppressed patients is MOST commonly caused by 20.____

A. cytomegalovirus
B. influenza virus type A
C. para influenza virus
D. respiratory syncitial virus

21. Priorities for planning nursing care of patients with pneumonia include treatment of the infection, maintenance of adequate oxygenation, and maintenance of patent airways. While observing for evidence of complications, such as respiratory failure, appropriate outcome criteria include all of the following EXCEPT 21.____

A. breath sounds clear with coughing
B. PaO_2 less than 55 mmHg at rest and with activities
C. sputum expectorated with minimal effort
D. appetite returns to normal baseline

22. Tuberculosis can be highly contagious and is transmitted by airborne mechanisms from infected persons. 22.____
The one of the following which is NOT a common cause of tuberculosis is

A. mycobacterium tuberculosis
B. M. bovis
C. M. leprae
D. M. africanum

23. Patients at INCREASED risk for drug-resistant tuberculosis include 23.____

A. foreign-born persons from Asia, Africa, and Latin America
B. persons with positive bacteriology after 3 months of therapy
C. contacts of known or suspected drug-resistant cases
D. all of the above

24. Lung cancer is a serious health problem in the United States. 24.____
Risk factors for lung cancer include all of the following EXCEPT

A. cigarette smoking
B. amphetamine abuse
C. asbestos exposure
D. exposure to arsenic, radon, and chromium

25. Hematological manifestations associated with lung cancer include 25.____

    A. anemia
    B. disseminated intravascular coagulation
    C. thrombophlebitis
    D. all of the above

KEY (CORRECT ANSWERS)

1. C
2. B
3. D
4. A
5. C

6. B
7. C
8. A
9. C
10. A

11. B
12. D
13. D
14. A
15. C

16. D
17. C
18. C
19. B
20. A

21. B
22. C
23. D
24. B
25. D

EXAMINATION SECTION
TEST 1

DIRECTIONS: Each question or incomplete statement is followed by several suggested answers or completions. Select the one that BEST answers the question or completes the statement. *PRINT THE LETTER OF THE CORRECT ANSWER IN THE SPACE AT THE RIGHT.*

Questions 1-10.

DIRECTIONS: Questions 1 through 10 are to be answered on the basis of the following information.

Fifty-year-old George Hoffman works in the basement of a garment factory. All of a sudden, he starts losing consciousness. An ambulance is called, and he is taken to the emergency room of the nearest hospital.

During the initial examination in the emergency room, he is found to have rapid, shallow breathing, non-palpable pulses over major vessels, and absent heart sounds.

1. Of the following, the MOST likely nursing diagnosis for this patient is 1.____

   A. arteriosclerosis
   B. cardiopulmonary arrest
   C. restrictive cardiomyopathy
   D. endocarditis

2. The nursing intervention of HIGHEST priority after receiving George in the emergency room would be 2.____

   A. to administer dopamine and norepinephrine to treat for shock
   B. to administer calcium chloride to help heartbeat
   C. defibrillation
   D. CPR

3. All of the following would be part of George's drug therapy EXCEPT 3.____

   A. lidocaine and procainamide
   B. epinephrine
   C. penicillin G
   D. sodium bicarbonate

4. While assessing George, the nurse probably does NOT expect to notice 4.____

   A. pallor
   B. dilation of pupils
   C. ventricular fibrillation
   D. petechiae and edema

5. George is unconscious. In an unconscious person, the relaxed tongue and neck muscles fail to lift the tongue from the posterior pharyngeal wall, blocking the hypo-pharyngeal airway. The nurse applies a basic head tilt maneuver to open the patient's airway, but does not receive a positive response.
   Additional measures which may then be used by the nurse to open the airway include 5.____

   A. head tilt-chin lift
   B. head tilt-neck lift
   C. mandibular jaw thrust
   D. all of the above

6. George is also found to have suffered cervical spine injury as a result of falling. The nurse should know that _______ is absolutely contra-indicated in the presence of cervical spine injury. 6._____

   A. direct current defibrillation
   B. external cardiac compression
   C. backward head tilt
   D. all of the above

7. In single-rescuer CPR, the nurse would give 2 breaths (1 to 1.5 sec. each) after each cycle of _______ cardiac compressions, delivered at a rate of 80 to 100/minute. 7._____

   A. 5 B. 10 C. 15 D. 20

8. All of the following would be important and appropriate nursing interventions to save George's life EXCEPT: 8._____

   A. Begin precordial thump and, if successful, administer calcium chloride
   B. If precordial thump is unsuccessful, perform defibrillation
   C. If defibrillation is unsuccessful, initiate CPR immediately
   D. Assist with administration of and monitor effects of additional emergency drugs

9. In 2-rescuer CPR, one ventilation (1.5 to 2 sec.) should be given after each cycle of _______ cardiac compressions, delivered at a rate of 80 to 100/minute. 9._____

   A. 5 B. 10 C. 15 D. 20

10. Which of the following drugs is used as the standard therapy for ventricular fibrillation (VF) or ventricular tachycardia (VT), and is used with countershock to convert VF? 10._____

   A. Procainamide
   B. Bretylium tosylate
   C. Lidocaine
   D. Epinephrine

Questions 11-20.

DIRECTIONS: Questions 11 through 20 are to be answered on the basis of the following information.

52-year-old John Goodman is brought to the emergency room by his wife with complaints of fever, cough, upper quadrant pain, and joint pain. Mrs. Goodman informs the health care team that John has also been losing weight.

11. John has been diagnosed with infective endocarditis. Mrs. Goodman has no knowledge about this disease, so she anxiously asks the nurse about it. The nurse explains to Mrs. Goodman that infective endocarditis is a(n) 11._____

   A. inflammation of the parietal pericardium caused by a viral infection
   B. accumulation of fluid in the pericardium that prevents adequate ventricular filling, caused by a fungal infection
   C. microbial infection of the endocardium which may result in valvular incompetence or obstruction, myocardial abscess, or mycotic aneurysm
   D. formation of platelet and fibrin thrombi on cardiac valves and the adjacent endocardium in response to bacterial infection

12. Which of the following bacterias is among the common causes of infection in endocarditis? 12.____

    A. S. aureus
    B. S. viridans
    C. B. hemolytic streptococcus and gonococcus
    D. All of the above

13. While assessing John, the nurse expects to find all of the following EXCEPT 13.____

    A. malaise and fatigue
    B. edema
    C. elevated WBC and ESR
    D. increased Hgb and Hct

14. As a clinical manifestation, the symptom found in John that is NOT secondary to emboli is _______ pain. 14.____

    A. upper left quadrant
    B. flank
    C. joint
    D. chest

15. All of the following medications will be part of John's drug therapy EXCEPT 15.____

    A. epinephrine, to enhance endocardial contractile force
    B. antibiotics specific to the sensitivity of the organism cultured
    C. penicillin G and streptomycin, if the organism is not known
    D. antipyretics

16. In order for John to maintain homeostasis and avoid complications over long-term hospitalization, the one of the following things a nurse does NOT have to do is 16.____

    A. administer antibiotics as ordered
    B. control temperature elevation by administration of antipyretics
    C. evaluate for complications of emboli and congestive heart failure
    D. record baseline blood pressure in three positions, i.e., lying, sitting, and standing, in both arms

17. To isolate the etiologic agent, the nurse would perform _______ blood cultures of _______ mL each within 24 hours. 17.____

    A. 1 to 3; 10 to 20
    B. 3 to 5; 20 to 30
    C. 5 to 7; 10 to 20
    D. 3 to 5; 15 to 20

18. All of the following factors are associated with poor prognosis of infective endocarditis EXCEPT 18.____

    A. heart failure
    B. delay in initiating therapy
    C. young age
    D. major embolic events

19. Even after successful antimicrobial therapy, John will be at risk of sterile emboli and valve rupture for 19.____

    A. 6 months
    B. 1 year
    C. 1 1/2 years
    D. 2 years

20. John has recovered and is now ready to be discharged from the hospital. While discussing discharge planning, the nurse would instruct John and his wife regarding all of the following EXCEPT 20.____

    A. types of procedures or treatments that increase the chances of recurrence
    B. antifungal therapy, including name, purpose, dose, frequency, and side effects
    C. signs and symptoms of recurrent endocarditis
    D. avoidance of individuals with known infections

Questions 21-30.

DIRECTIONS: Questions 21 through 30 are to be answered on the basis of the following information.

54-year-old Donna Smith is brought to the hospital's emergency room by her husband after having fever, malaise, and chest pain aggravated by breathing and swallowing.

21. After being examined by the physician, Donna is diagnosed with pericarditis. Mr. Smith asks the nurse about the nature of this disease. The nurse tells him that pericarditis is 21.____

    A. an accumulation of fluid or blood in the pericardium that prevents adequate ventricular filling, caused by a fungal infection
    B. an inflammation of the visceral and parietal pericardium, caused by a bacterial, viral, or fungal infection
    C. the formation of platelet and fibrin thrombi on cardiac valves and the adjacent pericardium in response to bacterial infection
    D. none of the above

22. Acute pericarditis may be a manifestation of all of the following EXCEPT 22.____

    A. rheumatoid arthritis
    B. systemic lupus erythematosus
    C. hemochromatosis
    D. scleroderma

23. Commonly used drugs that may produce acute pericarditis do NOT include 23.____

    A. procainamide
    B. hydralazine
    C. isoniazid
    D. lidocaine

24. Common causes of pericarditis include 24.____

    A. tuberculosis
    B. streptococcal infections
    C. staphylococcal infection
    D. all of the above

25. A scratchy, leathery sound heard in both systole and diastole is the CLASSIC sign of acute pericarditis known as 25.____

    A. pericardial friction rub
    B. epicardial rub friction
    C. myocardial friction rub
    D. dip and plateau

26. During Donna's assessment, the nurse does NOT expect to notice 26.____

    A. cough and hemoptysis
    B. tachycardia and pulsus paradoxus
    C. cyanosis or pallor
    D. decreased WBC and ESR

27. Which of the following is INCORRECT regarding Donna's drug therapy? It 27.____

    A. is medication for pain relief
    B. includes corticosteroids, salicylates, and indometha-cin
    C. includes calcium chloride
    D. is specific antibiotic therapy against the causative organism

28. The FALSE statement regarding chronic pericarditis is: 28.____

    A. It may be serous, fibrous, adhesive, hemorrhagic, purulent, fibrinous, or calcific
    B. It is asymptomatic unless constrictive pericarditis is present
    C. Coagulants are usually contraindicated in pericardial disease
    D. As a general treatment, meperidine 50 to 100 mg orally or IM may be given q 4 hours for pain

29. All of the following are proper nursing interventions to control Donna's condition EXCEPT 29.____

    A. ensuring comfort: bedrest with semi or high-Fowler's position
    B. monitoring hemodynamic parameters carefully
    C. administering medications as ordered and monitoring effects
    D. assessing for vascular complications

30. Donna has recovered and is now ready to be discharged. During the discharge planning conference, the nurse would probably NOT advise Mr. and Mrs. Smith about 30.____

    A. signs and symptoms of pericarditis indicative of a recurrence
    B. medication regimen including name, purpose, dosage, frequency, and side effects
    C. keeping all the emergency medications available at all times
    D. none of the above

KEY (CORRECT ANSWERS)

1. B
2. D
3. C
4. D
5. D

6. C
7. C
8. A
9. A
10. C

11. C
12. D
13. D
14. C
15. A

16. D
17. B
18. C
19. B
20. B

21. B
22. C
23. D
24. D
25. A

26. D
27. C
28. C
29. D
30. A

TEST 2

DIRECTIONS: Each question or incomplete statement is followed by several suggested answers or completions. Select the one that BEST answers the question or completes the statement. *PRINT THE LETTER OF THE CORRECT ANSWER IN THE SPACE AT THE RIGHT.*

Questions 1-10.

DIRECTIONS: Questions 1 through 10 are to be answered on the basis of the following information.

52-year-old Tim Brown visits his doctor after suffering for the last 3 days from pain in his legs and feet and numbness and tingling of the toes, and noticing shiny and taut skin with hair loss on his lower legs.

1. After being examined by the physician, Tim is diagnosed with arteriosclerosis obliterans. The nurse, after being asked by Tim about the disease, explains to him that arteriosclerosis obliterans is a chronic occlusive ______ disease that may affect the ______ . 1.____

   A. arterial; inferior vena cava or the extremities
   B. venous; superior vena cava or the extremities
   C. venous; pulmonary vessels or the extremities
   D. arterial; abdominal aorta or the lower extremities

2. The obstruction of blood flow with resultant ischemia usually does NOT affect the ______ artery. 2.____

   A. femoral
   B. aortal
   C. oesophageal
   D. iliac

3. Arteriosclerosis obliterans occurs MOST often in ______ ages ______ . 3.____

   A. men; 40-50
   B. women; 40-50
   C. men; 50-60
   D. women; 50-60

4. Which of the following is NOT a risk factor for arteriosclerosis obliterans? 4.____

   A. Hypotension
   B. Cigarette smoking
   C. Hyperlipidemia
   D. Diabetes mellitus

5. While assessing Mr. Brown, the nurse expects to notice all of the following EXCEPT 5.____

   A. both intermittent claudication and rest pain
   B. pallor after 1-2 minutes of elevating feet
   C. diminished or absent radial pulse
   D. diminished or absent dorsalis pedis pulse

6. The one of the following that is NOT a diagnostic test for arteriosclerosis obliterans is 6.____

   A. oscillometry
   B. seriology
   C. angiography
   D. doppler ultrasound

7. Mr. Brown is tired of staying in his bed and wants to walk around. 7.____
The nurse's BEST advice for him would be that he can

A. not do any physical activity until he is completely recovered and discharged from the hospital
B. leave his bed not more than once a day
C. leave his bed twice a day but not leave the room
D. leave his bed 3-4 times a day and walk twice a day

8. All of the following would be appropriate nursing interventions for Mr. Brown's recovery EXCEPT to 8.____

A. assess for sensory function and trophic changes
B. encourage slow, progressive physical activity
C. order medications as required
D. protect the patient from injury

9. Which of the following would NOT be appropriate teaching and discharge planning for the nurse to provide to Mr. Brown? 9.____
The importance of

A. a restricted kcal, high-saturated fat diet
B. continuing with established exercise program
C. avoiding constrictive clothing and standing in any position for a long time
D. foot care, immediately taking care of cuts, wounds, and injuries

10. Doppler ultrasound is the most widely used method in arteriosclerosis obliterans. 10.____
The SIMPLEST method for estimating blood flow to the lower extremities is to measure the ______ blood pressure at the level of the ankle and compare it to the ______ pressure.

A. systolic; brachial diastolic
B. diastolic; brachial diastolic
C. systolic; brachial systolic
D. systolic; femoral systolic

Questions 11-19.

DIRECTIONS: Questions 11 through 19 are to be answered on the basis of the following information,

32-year-old George Dawson visits the hospital after continuously experiencing coldness, tingling, numbness, and burning in all his extremities and, lately, getting an ulceration in one of his digits. Mr. Dawson is also a cigarette smoker.

11. After being examined by the physician, Mr. Dawson is diagnosed with thromboangiitis obliterans. 11.____
Thromboangiitis obliterans is BEST defined as an

A. acute, inflammatory disorder affecting small size arteries of the lower extremities
B. obliterative disease characterized by inflammatory changes in medium sized veins of the lower extremities
C. acute, inflammatory disorder affecting large sized arteries of the lower extremities
D. obliterative disease characterized by inflammatory changes in small and medium sized arteries and veins

12. The symptoms and signs of thromboangiitis obliterans are those of arterial ischemia and of superficial phlebitis. A history of migratory phlebitis, usually in the veins of the foot or leg, is present in ______ % of cases. 12.____

A. 20 B. 30 C. 40 D. 50

13. Thromboangiitis obliterans occurs MOST often in ______ ages ______ . 13.____

A. men; 35-50
B. women; 35-50
C. men; 25-40
D. women; 25-40

14. While assessing Mr. Dawson, the nurse expects to find all of the following EXCEPT 14.____

A. intermittent claudication
B. an increased posterior tibial pulse
C. trophic changes
D. ulceration and gangrene

15. ______ is NOT a diagnostic test for thromboangiitis obliterans. 15.____

A. Angiography
B. Contrast venography
C. Oscillometry
D. Doppler ultrasound

16. Which of the following would NOT be included among the appropriate nursing interventions to control Mr. Dawson's disease? 16.____

A. Prepare the patient for surgery when required
B. Provide vasodilators and analgesics as ordered
C. Administer coagulants not more than once a day
D. All of the above

17. All of the following are appropriate teaching and discharge information which should be provided by the nurse to Mr. Dawson EXCEPT the 17.____

A. drug regimen, including names, dosages, frequency, and side effects
B. need to avoid trauma to the affected extremity
C. need to avoid heat and have a good airconditioner in the bedroom
D. importance of stopping smoking

18. The only REALLY effective treatment for thromboangiitis obliterans is 18.____

A. antibiotics
B. corticosteroids
C. anticoagulants
D. cessation of smoking

19. In thromboangiitis obliterans, since the adventitia is usually more extensively infiltrated with fibroblasts, older lesions show periarterial fibrosis, which may involve the adjacent 19.____

A. artery
B. vein
C. nerve
D. all of the above

Questions 20-30.

DIRECTIONS: Questions 20 through 30 are to be answered on the basis of the following information.

30 year-old Sara Johnson got married six years ago. She never became pregnant, having used oral contraceptives. Now she visits the hospital after experiencing anxiety, fever, and chest pain.

20. After being examined by the physician, she is diagnosed with pulmonary embolism, which is BEST described as a(n) 20.____

    A. embolic obstruction to blood flow increasing venous pressure in the pulmonary artery and pulmonary hypotension
    B. embolic obstruction to blood flow involving the upper lobes of the lung because of higher blood flow
    C. lodgement of a blood clot in a pulmonary artery with subsequent obstruction of blood supply to the lung parenchyma
    D. lodgement of a blood clot in a pulmonary vein with subsequent obstruction of blood supply to the lung parenchyma

21. MOST pulmonary emboli arise as detached portions of venous thrombi formed in the 21.____

    A. deep veins of the legs
    B. right side of the heart
    C. pelvic area
    D. all of the above

22. Once released into the venous circulation, emboli are distributed to both lungs in about _______ % of cases, to the right lung in _______ % of cases, and to the left lung in _______ % of cases. 22.____

    A. 45; 40; 30
    B. 55; 30; 20
    C. 65; 20; 10
    D. 75; 10; 5

23. _______ lobes are involved in pulmonary embolism _______ times more often than _______ lobes. 23.____

    A. lower; 2; upper
    B. upper; 2; lower
    C. lower; 4; upper
    D. upper; 4; lower

24. Which of the following is NOT a risk factor for Mrs. Johnson? 24.____

    A. Trauma
    B. Pregnancy
    C. Oral contraceptives
    D. Intrauterine contraceptive devices

25. While assessing Mrs. Johnson, the nurse expects to notice all of the following EXCEPT 25.____

    A. severe dyspnea and a feeling of impending doom
    B. tachypnea and bradycardia
    C. increased pH due to hyperventilation
    D. crackles due to intensified pulmonic S_2

26. Concerning the diagnosis of pulmonary embolism, it is NOT correct that 26.____

    A. pulmonary arteriography reveals location and/or extent of embolism
    B. lung scan reveals adequacy or inadequacy of pulmonary circulation
    C. clinical symptoms and signs should suggest the diagnosis
    D. none of the above

27. All of the following drugs would be used in drug therapy for Mrs. Johnson EXCEPT 27.____

    A. anticoagulants
    B. dextran 70 to decrease viscosity and aggregation of blood cells
    C. narcotics for pain relief
    D. vasodepressors in the presence of shock

28. The surgical procedure used for the correction of pulmonary embolism is known as 28.____

    A. pulmonary thrombolectomy
    B. cardiac embolectomy
    C. pulmonary embolectomy
    D. cardiac thrombolectomy

29. It would be appropriate for the nurse attending to Mrs. Johnson to do all of the following EXCEPT 29.____

    A. administer oxygen therapy to correct hypoxemia
    B. provide adequate hydration to prevent hypocoagulability
    C. elevate the head of the bed to relieve dyspnea
    D. assist with turning, coughing, deep breathing, and passive ROM exercises

30. Which of the following is NOT considered among the appropriate teaching and discharge planning provided by the nurse to Mrs. Johnson? 30.____

    A. Use of plastic stockings when ambulatory
    B. Need to avoid sitting or standing for long periods of time
    C. Drug regimen
    D. Gradually increase walking distance

KEY (CORRECT ANSWERS)

1.	D	16.	C
2.	C	17.	C
3.	C	18.	D
4.	A	19.	D
5.	C	20.	C
6.	B	21.	D
7.	D	22.	C
8.	C	23.	C
9.	A	24.	D
10.	C	25.	B
11.	D	26.	D
12.	C	27.	D
13.	C	28.	C
14.	B	29.	B
15.	B	30.	A

EXAMINATION SECTION
TEST 1

DIRECTIONS: Each question or incomplete statement is followed by several suggested answers or completions. Select the one that BEST answers the question or completes the statement. *PRINT THE LETTER OF THE CORRECT ANSWER IN THE SPACE AT THE RIGHT.*

Questions 1-10.

DIRECTIONS: Questions 1 through 10 are to be answered on the basis of the following information.

Newly delivered, 34-year-old Susan Robinson comes to the hospital after feeling pain and noticing swollen, dilated, and tortuous skin veins in her lower extremities.

1. The physican examines Mrs. Robinson and makes a diagnosis of varicose veins, which is BEST described as elongated, dilated, tortuous superficial veins whose valves _______ , the condition occurring most often in the _______. 1.____

   A. are congenitally absent; lower extremities
   B. are scant; upper extremities
   C. have become incompetent; trunk
   D. are congenitally absent, scant, or have become incompetent; lower extremities and trunk

2. Varicose veins are MOST commonly found in _______ ages _______. 2.____

   A. women; 40 to 60
   B. men; 40 to 60
   C. women; 30 to 50
   D. both men and women; 30 to 50

3. All of the following are known to be predisposing factors for varicose veins EXCEPT 3.____

   A. congenital weakness of the veins
   B. obesity
   C. liver disease
   D. pregnancy

4. While assessing Mrs. Robinson, the nurse will NOT expect to notice 4.____

   A. pain after prolonged standing
   B. pain relieved by elevation
   C. tortuous skin veins
   D. deep, swollen and dilated veins

5. Which of the following would be used as a diagnostic test for Mrs. Robinson? 5.____

   A. X-rays
   B. Venography
   C. Plethysmography
   D. The Trendelenburg test

6. The one of the following that is NOT considered among the treatments for varicose veins is 6.____

   A. venography
   B. vein ligation
   C. injection sclerotherapy
   D. lightweight compression hosiery for small, mildly symptomatic varicose veins

7. All of the following would be appropriate nursing interventions for Mrs. Robinson EXCEPT 7.____

   A. measuring the circumference of the ankle and calf at least every 8 hours
   B. elevating legs above heart level
   C. applying knee-length elastic stockings
   D. providing adequate rest

8. It would NOT be an appropriate nursing intervention for vein ligation to 8.____

   A. keep the affected extremity above the level of the heart to prevent edema
   B. apply elastic bandages and stockings, which should be removed every 4 hours for short periods and reap-plied
   C. assist the patient out of bed within 24 hours, ensuring that elastic stockings are applied
   D. assess for increased bleeding, particularly in the groin area

9. Which of the following would NOT be part of the teaching and discharge planning provided by the nurse to Mrs. Robinson? 9.____
   Instruction regarding the

   A. importance of planned rest periods with elevation of the feet
   B. importance of adequate hydration to prevent hyper-coagulability
   C. need to avoid crossing the legs at the knees
   D. use of elastic stockings when on bed rest

10. All of the following statements about *spider veins* are correct EXCEPT: 10.____

   A. They are fine, intracutaneous angiectases of no serious consequence, but may be extensive and unsightly
   B. They are mostly symptomatic with patients' common complaints of burning and pain
   C. They can usually be eliminated by intracapillary injections of 1% solution of sodium tetradecyl sulfate through a fine-bore needle
   D. Best results are obtained by treating the whole leg at the initial visit and applying a compression bandage on the leg with ambulation for at least 3 weeks after treatment

Questions 11-18.

DIRECTIONS: Questions 11 through 18 are to be answered on the basis of the following information.

35-year-old Linda Gray comes to the hospital emergency room complaining of dizziness, weakness, and cold sensitivity after having excessive menses.

11. After a careful examination by the physician, Mrs. Gray is diagnosed with iron-deficiency anemia. Which of the following statements does NOT provide correct information about this disease? 11.____

   A. This is a chronic, microcytic, hypochromic anemia caused by either inadequate absorption or excessive loss of iron.
   B. Acute or chronic bleeding is the principal cause in adults resulting chiefly from trauma, excessive menses, and gastrointestinal bleeding.
   C. It can be caused by chronic diarrhea, malabsorption syndromes, and high cereal product intake with high animal protein ingestion.
   D. In iron-deficiency states, iron stores are depleted first, followed by a reduction in Hgb formation.

12. The incidence of iron-deficiency anemia is related to 12.____

   A. geographic location
   B. economic class
   C. age group and sex
   D. all of the above

13. The population affected MOST frequently by iron-deficiency anemia is 13.____

   A. women between ages 20-50
   B. men between ages 25-55
   C. children of all ages
   D. women between ages 15-45 and children

14. While assessing Mrs. Gray, the nurse expects to notice all of the following EXCEPT 14.____

   A. palpitations, dizziness, and cold sensitivity
   B. brittleness of hair and nails and pallor
   C. dysphagia, pruritis, and atrophic glossitis
   D. dyspnea and weakness

15. Which of the following is NOT a correct laboratory finding for iron-deficiency anemia? 15.____

   A. Red blood cells small (microcytic) and pale (hypo-chromic)
   B. Hemosiderin absent from bone marrow
   C. Hgb markedly decreased
   D. Reticulocyte count increased

16. All of the following would be appropriate nursing interventions for Mrs. Gray EXCEPT: 16.____

   A. Monitoring for signs and symptoms of bleeding through a hematest of pulmonary contents
   B. Providing for adequate rest and planning activities so as not to overtire
   C. Providing a thorough explanation of all diagnostic tests used to determine sources of possible bleeding, as it helps allay anxiety and ensure cooperation
   D. Monitoring for signs and symptoms of bleeding through a hematest of stool, urine, and gastric contents

17. It would NOT be an appropriate nursing intervention regarding oral iron preparations to 17.____

A. use oral iron preparations as the route of choice, recommended to be given following meals or a snack
B. dilute liquid preparations well and administer them using a straw to prevent staining teeth
C. administer with orange juice when possible, as vitamin C (ascorbic acid) enhances iron absorption
D. warn the patient that iron preparations will make stool color darker and may cause diarrhea

18. Concerning the use of parenteral iron preparations, do NOT 18.____

A. use them in patients intolerant to oral preparations, patients who have no complaints with therapy, or patients who have continuing blood losses
B. use one needle to withdraw and another to administer iron preparations, as tissue staining and irritation are problems
C. use the *Y* track injection technique to prevent leakage into tissues
D. massage the injection site, but encourage ambulation, as this will enhance absorption; advise against vigorous exercise and constricting garments

Questions 19-30.

DIRECTIONS: Questions 19 through 30 are to be answered on the basis of the following information.

58-year-old John Lithgow is brought to the hospital by his wife after suffering from weakness, sore mouth, diarrhea, and jaundice.

19. After being carefully examined by the physician, John is diagnosed with pernicious anemia, which is correctly explained by all of the following statements EXCEPT: 19.____

A. It is a chronic, progressive, macrocytic anemia caused by a deficiency of intrinsic factor; the result is abnormally large erythrocytes and hypo-chlorhydria
B. It is characterized by neurologic and gastrointestinal symptoms; death usually results if it goes untreated
C. A lack of intrinsic factor is caused by gastric mucosal atrophy, possibly due to heredity, prolonged iron deficiency, or an autoimmune disorder
D. It can result in patients who have had a total gastrec-tomy if vitamin B_2 is not administered

20. It is NOT a true pathophysiological finding about pernicious anemia that 20.____

A. an intrinsic factor is necessary for the absorption of vitamin B_{12} by the large intestine
B. b_{12} deficiency diminishes DNA synthesis, which results in defective maturation of cells, particularly rapidly dividing cells such as blood cells and gastrointestinal tract cells
C. B_{12} deficiency can alter structure and function of peripheral nerves
D. B_{12} deficiency can alter structure and function of the spinal cord and the brain

21. While assessing John, the nurse may expect to notice all of the following EXCEPT 21.____

A. pallor, dyspnea, palpitations, and fatigue
B. sore mouth with smooth, beefy, red tongue
C. tingling, paresthesias of hands and feet and paralysis
D. depression, hypertension, and psychosis

22. The one of the following that will NOT show up on a laboratory test of pernicious anemia is 22.____

A. decreased erythrocyte count
B. blood smear showing oval, macrocytic erythrocytes with a proportionate amount of Hgb
C. very small numbers of reticulocytes in the blood following parenteral vitamin B_{12} administration
D. elevated serum LDH

23. Which of the following statements is NOT true about the positive Schilling test? It 23.____

A. measures absorption of radioactive vitamin B_{12} before parenteral administration of intrinsic factor
B. measures absorption of radioactive vitamin B_{12} after parenteral administration of extrinsic factor
C. is a definitive test for pernicious anemia
D. is used to detect lack of intrinsic factor

24. All of the following will be part of John's drug therapy EXCEPT 24.____

A. monthly maintenance by vitamin B_{12} injections
B. iron preparations if Hgb level is inadequate to meet increased number of erythrocytes
C. folic acid
D. folic acid, which is safe if given in large amounts in addition to vitamin B_{12}

25. A 1000 mg injection of vitamin B_{12} can be given IM ______ times per week until hematologic abnormalities are corrected; then it is given once monthly. 25.____

A. 2
B. 3
C. 4
D. all of the above

26. A nurse should provide all of the following to control John's condition EXCEPT 26.____

A. mouth care before and after meals using a hard toothbrush for better cleansing and non-irritating rinses
B. a nutritious diet high in iron, protein, and vitamins such as fish, meat, milk/milk products, and eggs
C. teaching concerning dietary instructions and the importance of lifelong vitamin B_{12} therapy
D. bedrest if anemia is severe

27. Folic acid administration to anyone in the B_{12}-deprived state is contraindicated since it may result in fulminant ______ deficit. 27.____

A. renal
B. hepatic
C. neurologic
D. all of the above

28. Pernicious anemia MOST commonly occurs in 28.____

A. men over age 50
B. women over age 50
C. blue-eyed persons of Scandinavian descent
D. all of the above

29. Which of the following statements is FALSE about the Schilling test? 29.____

A. Schilling III can be done after a 2-week trial of oral tetracycline.
B. Labeled urine collection will contain less than 9% of the administered dose.
C. Decreased excretion of radiolabeled B_{12} and normal excretion of labeled B_{12} bound to intrinsic factor establishes a defect in intrinsic factor production.
D. Since the test provides 612 repletion, it should be performed after completion of all studies and planned therapeutic trials.

30. Which of the following is NOT considered a correct laboratory diagnosis finding for pernicious anemia? 30.____

A. The anemia is macrocytic, with an MCV less than 100.
B. In general, low values of less than 150 pg/mL are reliable indications of vitamin B_{12} deficiency.
C. In borderline circumstances, i.e., 150-250 pg/mL, clinical judgment and other tests must supplement the radioassay.
D. Autoantibodies to gastric parietal cells can be identified in 80 to 90% of patients with pernicious anemia and antibodies to intrinsic factor can be found in the sera of most of these patients.

KEY (CORRECT ANSWERS)

1. D
2. D
3. C
4. D
5. D

6. A
7. A
8. B
9. D
10. B

11. C
12. D
13. D
14. C
15. D

16. A
17. D
18. C
19. D
20. A

21. D
22. C
23. B
24. D
25. D

26. A
27. C
28. D
29. B
30. A

TEST 2

DIRECTIONS: Each question or incomplete statement is followed by several suggested answers or completions. Select the one that BEST answers the question or completes the statement. *PRINT THE LETTER OF THE CORRECT ANSWER IN THE SPACE AT THE RIGHT.*

1. In which of the following groups of people is stomach cancer MOST frequently found? 1.____

   A. Spanish
   B. Japanese
   C. White Americans
   D. Black Americans

2. A patient who is severely allergic to penicillin has streptococcal pharyngitis. 2.____
   The drug of choice is

   A. vancomycin
   B. tetracyline
   C. erythromycin
   D. sulfonamide

3. A 20-year-old male has gonococcal urethritis proven by a culture. 3.____
   The drug of choice to treat him is

   A. penicillin
   B. erythromycin
   C. ceftriaxon
   D. sulfonamide

4. Hookworm disease can be prevented by 4.____

   A. inspecting meat
   B. washing hands
   C. sterilizing water supply
   D. wearing shoes

5. Pulmonary fibrosis is an adverse side effect of the anti-cancer medication 5.____

   A. adriamycin
   B. vincristin
   C. cyclophosphomide
   D. bleomycin

6. A 25-year-old male is treated with methecillin for staphy-lococcus infection. Ten days later, the patient develops hematuria. 6.____
   The MOST likely diagnosis is

   A. membrano proliferative glomerulonephritis
   B. acute glomerulonephritis
   C. nephrotic syndrome
   D. allergic nephritis

7. A 20-year-old male's exudative tonsilopharyngitis was treated with ampicillin, after which he developed generalized rash and hepatosplenomaly. 7.____
   What is the MOST likely diagnosis?

   A. Infectious mononucleosis
   B. Diphtheria
   C. Streptococcal pharyngitis
   D. Hemophilus influenzae pharyngitis

8. A 25-year-old woman has vaginal discharge and her vaginal culture is positive for chlamydia. 8.____
The treatment of choice is

A. penicillin
B. metronidazol
C. erythromycin
D. amphotericin B

Questions 9-17.

DIRECTIONS: Questions 9 through 17 are to be answered on the basis of the following information.

Sixty-year-old James Bond is brought to the emergency room by his wife after suffering from severe low abdominal and low back pain.

9. After being examined by the physician, Mr. Bond is diagnosed with an abdominal aortic aneurysm, which is BEST defined as a 9.____

A. saccular aneurysm developed above the renal arteries and caused by arteriosclerosis
B. dissecting aneurysm developed below the iliac bifurcation and caused by atherosclerosis
C. localized dilation of the aorta developing just above the iliac bifurcation caused by trauma
D. localized dilation of the abdominal aorta developing just below the renal arteries but above the iliac bifurcation caused by arteriosclerosis, atherosclerosis, hypertension, trauma, syphilis, or other types of infectious processes

10. Abdominal aortic aneurysm occurs MOST often in ______ ages ______. 10.____

A. men; 51-60
B. women; 51-60
C. men; 61 and over
D. women; 61 and over

11. Abdominal aortic aneurysms of arteriosclerosis commonly pass unnoticed until they become large enough to cause symptoms or to be felt as a pulsating mass of about ______ cm. 11.____

A. 2-4
B. 4-6
C. 6-8
D. 8-10

12. While assessing Mr. Bond, the nurse would expect to notice all of the following EXCEPT 12.____

A. severe mid to low abdominal pain and low back pain
B. mass in the periumbilical area or slightly to the left of the midline with bruits heard over the mass
C. pulsating abdominal mass
D. increased femoral pulses

13. ______ is(are) NOT used as a diagnostic test for an abdominal aortic aneurysm. 13.____

A. X-rays
B. Aortography
C. Venography
D. Ultrasound

14. Appropriate pre-operative nursing interventions for abdominal aortic aneurysms include 14.____

    A. preparing patient for surgery
    B. assessing rate and rhythm of peripheral pulses
    C. assessing character of the peripheral pulses
    D. all of the above

15. A nurse attending post-operatively to a patient with an abdominal aortic aneurysm does NOT have to 15.____

    A. make circulation checks noting rate, rhythm, and character of all pulses distal to the graft at least twice a day
    B. monitor hourly outputs through a Foley catheter
    C. keep the patient flat in bed without sharp flexion of the hip or knee
    D. prevent thrombophlebitis by encouraging the patient to dorsiflex his foot while in bed

16. All of the following would be part of the teaching and discharge planning provided by the nurse to Mr. Bond EXCEPT advice concerning the importance of 16.____

    A. changes in color or temperature of extremities
    B. avoidance of prolonged sitting, standing, and smoking
    C. a gradual progressive activity regimen
    D. adherence to a low cholesterol and a high-saturated fat diet

17. The MOST appropriate medical management for Mr. Bond's recovery would be 17.____

    A. injection sclerotherapy
    B. clinical monitoring of the indicators of shock
    C. surgical resection of the lesion and replacement with a graft
    D. chlorpromazine 10 to 25 mg orally q 6 to 8 hours

Questions 18-30.

DIRECTIONS: Questions 18 through 30 are to be answered on the basis of the following information.

48-year-old Marge Simpson has been working in a garment factory for the last ten years as a sewing machine operator 8 to 10 hours a day. She comes to the hospital after feeling pain and noticing tenderness and redness in one of her lower extremities. Marge is also a cigarette smoker.

18. After being examined by the physician, Marge is diagnosed with thrombophlebitis, which is BEST defined as the 18.____

    A. inflammation of the vessel walls of saphenous and femoral veins with formation of a thrombus
    B. inflammation of the walls of femoral and popliteal veins with formation of an embolus
    C. inflammation of the arterial wall with formation of a thrombus, the most frequently affected arteries being saphenous, femoral, and popliteal
    D. presence of a thrombus in a vein, most commonly in the saphenous, femoral, and popliteal veins

19. Which of the following factors may contribute to thrombophlebitis? 19.____

A. Injury to the epithelium of the vein
B. Hypercoagulability
C. Stasis
D. All of the above

20. The nurse knows that the terms phlegmasia alba dolens and phlegmesia cerulea dolens are applied to extensive thrombosis of the involved extremity depending on 20.____

A. what part of the extremity is involved
B. size of the involvement
C. its color
D. its temperature

21. Effort (strain) thrombosis occurs in the ______ veins,secondary to trauma to the vein in the thoracic outlet during unusual physical effort in which the arm is fully abducted. 21.____

A. esophageal
B. aortic
C. subclavian
D. pulmonary

22. The nurse would consider all of the following risk factors for Marge EXCEPT 22.____

A. cigarette smoking
B. intrauterine contraceptive devices
C. prolonged immobility
D. complications of surgery

23. The nurse, while assessing Marge, would NOT expect to notice 23.____

A. tenderness, redness, and induration along the course of the vein in the situation of superficial vein involvement
B. swelling, venous distension of the limb; tenderness and cyanosis in deep veins
C. elevated WBC and decreased ESR
D. positive Homan's sign in the situation of deep vein involvement

24. Regarding the anticoagulant therapy used for Marge, it is INCORRECT that 24.____

A. heparin blocks the conversion of prothrombin to thrombin and reduces the formation or extension of thrombus
B. side effects of heparin include spontaneous bleeding, ecchymosis, cyanosis, thrombocytopenia, and others
C. warfarin (coumadin) blocks prothrombin synthesis by interfering with vitamin D synthesis
D. side effects of warfarin include nausea and vomiting, diarrhea, urticaria, pruritis, transient hair loss, burning sensation of feet and others

25. All of the following are true concerning Marge's medical management by surgery EXCEPT: 25.____

A. A good prognosis of vein ligation
B. A contraindication of vein stripping
C. Venous thrombectomy; removal of a clot in the ilio-femoral region
D. Plication of the inferior vena cava; insertion of an umbrella-like prosthesis into the lumen of the vena cava to filter incoming clot

26. ______ would NOT be used as one of the diagnostic tests in the case of Marge. 26.____

A. Venography
B. Doppler ultrasonography
C. Plethysmography
D. The Trendelenburg test

27. A nurse treating Marge would NOT have to 27.____

A. provide bedrest, elevating the involved extremity to increase venous return and decrease edema
B. apply continuous warm, moist soaks to decrease lymphatic congestion
C. assess vital signs every 8 hours
D. monitor for chest pain or shortness of breath

28. When using heparin as an anticoagulant in thrombophlebitis, a nurse should do all of the following EXCEPT 28.____

A. recognize that one of the proper injection techniques is the use of 26- or 27-gauge tuberculin syringe with 1/2 - 5/8 in. needle, injected into the fatty layer of the abdomen below the iliac crest
B. monitor PTT; dosage should be adjusted to keep PTT between 1.5-2.5 times the normal control level
C. assess for increased bleeding tendencies and instruct the patient to observe for and report these
D. have an antidote (protamine sulfate) available

29. All of the following would be appropriate nursing interventions concerning use of warfarin (coumadin) as an anticoagulant in thrombophlebitis EXCEPT 29.____

A. obtaining careful medication history, as there are many drug-drug interactions
B. instructing patient to use a hard toothbrush and to floss regularly
C. having an antidote (vitamin K) available
D. instructing patient to wear Medic-Alert bracelet

30. It would NOT be appropriate teaching and discharge planning for the nurse to tell Marge to 30.____

A. avoid prolonged standing or sitting, constrictive clothing, smoking, and oral contraceptives
B. avoid physical activities, such as swimming
C. maintain adequate hydration to prevent hypercoagability
D. use of elastic stockings when ambulatory

KEY (CORRECT ANSWERS)

1.	B	16.	D
2.	C	17.	C
3.	C	18.	D
4.	D	19.	D
5.	D	20.	C
6.	D	21.	C
7.	A	22.	B
8.	C	23.	C
9.	D	24.	C
10.	C	25.	B
11.	B	26.	D
12.	D	27.	C
13.	C	28.	A
14.	D	29.	B
15.	A	30.	B

EXAMINATION SECTION
TEST 1

DIRECTIONS: Each question or incomplete statement is followed by several suggested answers or completions. Select the one that *BEST* answers the question or completes the statement. *PRINT THE LETTER OF THE CORRECT ANSWER IN THE SPACE AT THE RIGHT.*

1. If the label on the bottle of sodium bicarbonate reads "0.32 gm. in 4cc," when the dosage ordered is grs, XV, you *should* give 1.____

   A. 0.15 gm B. 0.20 gm C. 0.44 gm D. 0.96 gm

2. In preparing to administer morphine, sulfate gr 1/8 (h) from tablets 0.010 gm, the accurate dosage would be ______ tablet. 2.____

   A. 1/3 B. 1/2 C. 3/4 D. 4/5

3. If the label reads "Acetylsalicylic Acid 0.32 gm (grams)" for a 10-grain dosage, you should give ______ tablets. 3.____

   A. 2 B. 4 C. 5 D. 8

4. According to Young's Rule, a child of 8 years will receive ______ of the adult dosage. 4.____

   A. 2/5 B. 1/3 C. 1/2 D. 4/5

5. The dietary treatment of diabetes mellitus includes: 5.____

   A. Equalizing intake of proteins, carbohydrates, and fats
   B. Giving carbohydrates with restriction and adjusting intake of insulin
   C. Rigid restriction of carbohydrates and increased intake of fats
   D. Maintenance of body weight at optimal level

6. In cardiac disease, the purpose of the low sodium diet is to 6.____

   A. relieve edema
   B. increase kidney function by changing the salt balance
   C. reduce weight through decrease of appetite
   D. make sure that the patient is salt free

7. In fat-controlled diets, 7.____

   A. all fats are restricted
   B. fatty meats are restricted; dairy foods are unrestricted
   C. poly-unsaturated fats are substituted for saturated fats
   D. roast chicken is the preferred protein

8. Of the following, the procedure which *violates* a law of physics and increases fatigue is: 8.____

   A. Working with the patient in center of bed
   B. Carrying a basin of water close to body
   C. Carrying a basin by placing palms flat around the sides
   D. Standing with feet apart

9. The explanation of the fact that the comfort of the patient is related to the height of the headrest is: The ______ the headrest, the greater the ______. 9.____

A. *higher*; distribution of body weight
B. *lower*; distribution of body weight
C. *lower*; strain on the sacrum
D. *lower*; pressure on the buttocks

10. The "storage battery" which releases muscular energy instantly when a nerve impulse gives the order is a complex phosphate molecule commonly known as 10.____

A. FAO B. ATP C. WHO D. ITO

11. It is dangerous for a patient with a suspected malignancy of the gastro-intestinal tract to take sodium bicarbonate over an extended period of time because 11.____

A. it hastens calcium metastasis
B. its acidity is injurious to the tract lining
C. it interferes with secretion of bile
D. temporary relief pacifies the patient

12. The *approved* water temperature for the hot water bottle is: 12.____

A. 105 degrees F - 115 degrees F
B. 115 degrees F - 130 degrees F
C. 120 degrees F - 150 degrees F
D. 130 degrees F - 150 degrees F

13. Of the following items, the *one* that does *NOT* belong in the home medicine cabinet is 13.____

A. an antiseptic
B. a lubricant
C. a laxative
D. first-aid supplies

14. The value of the round-the-clock "q-4-h" temperature has been questioned because 14.____

A. temperature has become less important in the treatment of disease
B. it is known to vary with the time of day, month, age
C. it is known to vary with individuals
D. it wastes time of nursing personnel

15. Decubitus ulcers in bed-ridden patients are *BEST* avoided by the use of 15.____

A. plasticized rings
B. rubberized terry cotton draw sheets
C. sheepskin
D. polyurethane foam

16. The deciduous set of teeth does *NOT* contain 16.____

A. cuspids B. lateral incisors C. bicuspids D. canines

17. Adequate thermometer care is 17.____

A. soap, water, friction
B. aqueous zephiran
C. isoprophl alcohol 70%
D. alcohol 70%

KEY (CORRECT ANSWERS)

1. C
2. D
3. A
4. A
5. C
6. B
7. C
8. B
9. D
10. D
11. B
12. B
13. C
14. A
15. D
16. D
17. C
18. A
19. B
20. D
21. A
22. C
23. C
24. A
25. B

KEY (CORRECT ANSWERS)

1. D
2. D
3. C
4. A
5. D
6. A
7. C
8. A
9. B
10. B
11. D
12. B
13. C
14. A
15. D
16. C
17. A
18. C
19. C
20. B
21. B
22. A
23. B
24. C
25. B

TEST 2

DIRECTIONS: Each question or incomplete statement is followed by several suggested answers or completions. Select the one that *BEST* answers the question or completes the statement. *PRINT THE LETTER OF THE CORRECT ANSWER IN THE SPACE AT THE RIGHT.*

1. Radioactive carbon is a tracer element used to study the 1.____

   A. manufacture of erythrocytes
   B. motor nerve responses to stimuli
   C. path of certain food elements
   D. activity of certain endocrine glands

2. Mephenesin is used as a 2.____

   A. tranquillizer
   B. respiratory stimulant
   C. muscle relaxant
   D. respiratory depressant

3. Dextrostix are used as a one-minute test for sugar in the 3.____

   A. urine
   B. spinal fluid
   C. gastric juice
   D. blood

4. Cleft palate and hare lip have been developed in animals by depriving prospective animal mothers of certain vitamins during the period when the foetus' jaw and mouth are being formed. These vitamins are certain B vitamins *and* vitamin 4.____

   A. A
   B. C
   C. D
   D. E

5. Edathamil calcium disodium may be administered before brain damage occurs in cases of diagnosed 5.____

   A. phenylketonuria
   B. Wilson's disease
   C. lead poisoning
   D. secondary anemia

6. Eggs contain an emulsifier of cholesterol known as 6.____

   A. lysine
   B. lecithen
   C. acetylcholine
   D. trypsin

7. To ease the chronic shortage of high quality human bone available from bone bands, the Federal Drug Administration has approved the detailed processing of ______ bones. 7.____

   A. yearling lamb
   B. six-months-old lamb
   C. six-weeks-old calves'
   D. two-years-old cows'

8. The one-shot so-called "health gift" of measles vaccine contains ______ virus. 8.____

   A. dead measles
   B. live measles
   C. mixed dead
   D. mixed live

9. The diet prescribed for a phenylketonuria which may prevent brain damage is one that is 9.____

   A. *low* in fruits and vegetables, *high* in protein
   B. *high* in fruits, vegetables, and animal protein
   C. a commercially available protein substitute
   D. vegetables, fruits, and a commercially available protein substitute

10. The Haversian Canals are associated with the 10.____

A. secretion of anterior pituitary gland
B. aqueous humor in the eye
C. excretion of pancreatic juice
D. structure of long bones

11. A colles fracture is associated with the fracture of 11.____

A. the lower third of the tibia - fibula
B. the lower third of the radius
C. a lumbar vertebra
D. the upper third of the femus

12. In muscles undergoing contraction, irritability and fatigue may result from an accumulation of 12.____

A. phosphoric acid
B. carbon dioxide and lactic acid
C. glycogen
D. creatine

13. In the care of a patient who has suffered a cerebral vascular accident, the nurse's *FIRST* concern is 13.____

A. rehabilitation of the patient
B. helping to restore the confidence of the patient
C. survival of the patient
D. careful feeding

14. The procedure *MOST* frequently used to withdraw a small amount of spinal fluid for diagnosis is called a 14.____

A. lumbar puncture
B. cisternal puncture
C. pneumoencephalogram
D. ventriculogram

15. An infection of the kidney pelvis and the spread of the infection to the kidney tissue results in a condition known as 15.____

A. hydronephrosis
B. nephrosclerosis
C. nephritis
D. pyelonephritis

16. An *alternate* for insulin therapy in some cases of diabetes is therapy using 16.____

A. sulfadiazine
B. sulfaguanidine
C. sulfapyrimidine
D. sulfonylurea

17. When there is severe bleeding, it is usually *best* to IMMEDIATELY 17.____

A. apply a sterile dressing
B. apply a tourniquet
C. apply a pressure bandage
D. elevate the area

18. The *PRIMARY* function of protein in the body is to 18.____

A. supply material for growth and repair of body tissues
B. supply energy
C. aid in the proper utilization of other nutrients
D. transport vitamins and minerals to various parts of the body

19. *Good* diagnostic procedures used to give information about the heart are: 19.____

 A. Chest x-ray and electro-cardiogram
 B. Fluoroscopy and cardiac catheterization
 C. Lipiodal x-ray and B.M.R.
 D. Complete blood count and urinalysis

20. To avoid gastric irritation by frequent large doses of acetylsalicylic acid, the physician orders 20.____

 A. buffered tablets
 B. salicylic acid tablets
 C. aluminum hydroxide gel
 D. enteric coated tablets

21. The respiratory center is located in the 21.____

 A. medulla oblongata
 B. occipital lobe of the cerebrum
 C. corpus callosum
 D. cerebellum

22. The anatomical structure which performs the function of the nervous system is the 22.____

 A. neuroglia
 B. fibers of Remak
 C. neuron
 D. exteroceptors

23. Disruption of the erythrocyte membrane which leads to the cells' hemoglobin content going into solution in the plasma is known as 23.____

 A. agglutination
 B. phagocytosis
 C. hemolysis
 D. hemopoiesis

24. The cause of primary anemia is 24.____

 A. the inability of the patient to produce the erythrocyte maturation factor
 B. a poor nutritional pattern causing lack of hemoglobin
 C. sudden loss of large amounts of blood
 D. hereditary and may appear in any generation

25. Extensive superficial frostbite should be treated as deep frostbite, using a bacteriostatic agent and whirlpool bath of ______ water. 25.____

 A. cool
 B. warm
 C. hot
 D. cold

KEY (CORRECT ANSWERS)

1. C
2. D
3. A
4. A
5. C

6. B
7. C
8. B
9. D
10. D

11. B
12. B
13. C
14. A
15. D

16. D
17. C
18. A
19. B
20. D

21. A
22. C
23. C
24. A
25. B

EXAMINATION SECTION
TEST 1

DIRECTIONS: Each question or incomplete statement is followed by several suggested answers or completions. Select the one that *BEST* answers the question or completes the statement. *PRINT THE LETTER OF THE CORRECT ANSWER IN THE SPACE AT THE RIGHT.*

1. Neonatal respiratory distress in which the alveoli and the alveolar ducts are filled with a sticky exudate preventing aeration is known as 1.____

   A. caput succedaneum
   B. atelectasis
   C. cephalhematoma
   D. hyaline membrane disease

2. Concerning nutrition, the *PRIMARY* role of the nurse is to 2.____

   A. change the food patterns of the home
   B. help a patient follow the doctor's orders
   C. teach basic principles of food selection
   D. assist in food selection for the family

3. In an aortogram study of extracranial vessels, introduction of the catheter into the femoral artery is *preferable* because it visualizes 3.____

   A. external carotids and branches
   B. temporal artery and branches
   C. femoral artery and branches
   D. aortic artery and branches

4. The *CHIEF* substance used in aortography are compounds of 4.____

   A. Iodine
   B. Sulfa
   C. Silver
   D. Carbon

5. The technique for artificial respiration that has the advantage of providing pressure to inflate the victim's lungs *immediately* is the ______ method. 5.____

   A. back-pressure arm-lift
   B. chest-pressure arm-lift
   C. mouth-to-mouth
   D. prone-posture

6. Repeated attacks of hypoglycemia in diabetic children receiving insulin may produce 6.____

   A. acidosis
   B. brain damage
   C. diabetic coma
   D. ketosis

7. An antiviral protein produced by cells infected with virus which may prove to be an *effective* therapy in virus infections is 7.____

   A. beta globulin
   B. RNA
   C. gamma globulin
   D. interferon

8. The *DIRECT* source of muscle energy is 8.____

   A. potassium phosphate
   B. lactic acid
   C. sarcolactic acid
   D. phosphocreatin

9. The vitamin *essential* for the synthesis of prothrombin is 9.___

A. P B. B1 C. B6 D. K

10. Tubes containing radium are disinfected when necessary by 10.___

A. boiling to 212°
B. boiling to 250°
C. heat under pressure
D. chemical disinfection

11. The cardinal symptoms of erythroblastosis are: 11.___

A. Cherry red nail beds and coughing
B. Paroxysms of coughing and labored breathing
C. Jaundice and anemia
D. Dehydration and marked thirst

12. A hypertensive patient with cardiovascular-renal complications *usually* is advised to eat a ______ diet. 12.___

A. Meulengracht B. Brecht C. high sodium D. low sodium

13. Wilm's Tumor, often found in children, is a disease of the 13.___

A. brain B. kidney C. duodenum D. liver

14. In the phenylketonuric child, the diet must be limited in 14.___

A. phenolphthalein
B. phenylalanine
C. phenylhydrazine
D. phenylkania

15. A patient with a hemorrhage from a peptic ulcer is sometimes placed on a(n) ______ diet. 15.___

A. Andresen
B. gluten-free
C. low gelatin glucose
D. nutramigen

16. A *distinguishing* feature of the Jacksonian form of epilepsy is the 16.___

A. convulsive muscular behavior
B. involvement of only one side of the body
C. momentary lapse of consciousness
D. presence of psychic disturbances

17. Bacteriological sanitary analysis is made *PRIMARILY* to determine the presence of 17.___

A. colon bacillus
B. disease germs
C. nitrates
D. spore-forming bacteria

18. The *BEST* sources of the vitamin that is important to coagulation are: 18.___

A. Beef liver, calf liver, chicken liver
B. Cabbage, cauliflower, spinach
C. Corn, peas, yellow beans
D. Grapes, melon, pears

19. The *key* constituent of the thyroid hormone is 19.____

A. fluorine B. iodine C. chlorine D. thyrine

20. The *daily* requirement of thiamine for an adult is 20.____

A. related to the amount of carbohydrate being metabolized
B. 8.4 mg.
C. .006 mg.
D. related to the amount of fats being hydrolyzed

21. In liver diseases, such as infectious hepatitis, the diet must be modified to 21.____

A. *increase* roughage
B. *decrease* carbohydrates
C. *increase* fat content
D. *increase* protein intake

22. Distilled water added to a drop of blood on a slide will cause the erythrocytes to 22.____

A. agglutinate
B. crenate
C. shrivel
D. swell

23. Following early diagnosis of galactosemia, the health of the child is protected by keeping the diet *free* of 23.____

A. eggs B. meat C. milk D. potatoes

24. Friedman's Test is a 24.____

A. modification of the A-Z test
B. blood sugar tolerance test
C. renal function test
D. Vitamin K test

25. Aldosterone, the hormone essential for normal retention of sodium and excretion of potassium, is secreted by the 25.____

A. adrenal cortex
B. parathyroids
C. gonads
D. pituitary

KEY (CORRECT ANSWERS)

1. D
2. B
3. D
4. A
5. C

6. B
7. D
8. D
9. D
10. D

11. C
12. D
13. B
14. B
15. A

16. B
17. A
18. B
19. B
20. A

21. D
22. D
23. C
24. A
25. A

TEST 2

DIRECTIONS: Each question or incomplete statement is followed by several suggested answers or completions. Select the one that *BEST* answers the question or completes the statement. *PRINT THE LETTER OF THE CORRECT ANSWER IN THE SPACE AT THE RIGHT.*

1. The coat of viruses consists of 1.____

   A. enzymes
   B. nucleic acids
   C. polysaccharides
   D. protein

2. Of the following, the *one* that is *NOT* a symptom of radiation sickness is 2.____

   A. bleeding from mucous membranes
   B. breathing difficulty
   C. diarrhea
   D. sore throat

3. The rate of oxidation of alcohol in the body is 3.____

   A. accelerated by exercise
   B. fixed
   C. retarded by exercise
   D. retarded by sleep

4. A "broad-spectrum" antibiotic is 4.____

   A. bacitracin
   B. streptomycin
   C. chrysomycin
   D. aureomycin

5. If a virus were seen outside the living cell, it would appear to be 5.____

   A. non-living
   B. parasitic
   C. saprophytic
   D. toxic

6. Slight exposure to radioactive dust will cause 6.____

   A. destruction of germ cells
   B. destruction of brain tissue
   C. severe illness
   D. skin burns

7. A xanthine diuretic is 7.____

   A. caffeine
   B. calomel
   C. acetazolamide
   D. trichlormethiazide

8. An organism that grows rapidly in many foods and is the *MOST* common cause of gas-tro-intestinal infection is 8.____

   A. clostridium botulism
   B. dysentery bacillus
   C. salmonella
   D. streptococcus

9. Indiscriminate use of Vitamin D may lead to 9.____

   A. hearing loss
   B. excess bone calcification
   C. calcification of the arteries of the heart
   D. increase of the anti-menorrhagic factor in blood

10. In nutrition, increasing attention is being given to the importance of 10.____

A. carbohydrates
B. vitamins
C. minerals
D. amino acids

11. Sufferers from silcosis have turned increasingly to 11.____

A. streptomycin
B. chlorine gas
C. silicic acid
D. powdered aluminum

12. The medical term used to describe simple goiter is 12.____

A. simple adenoma
B. myxedema
C. colloid goiter
D. hyperthyroidism

13. What is considered to be the normal polymorphonuclear count? 13.____

A. 80 - 100% B. 70 - 80% C. 60 - 70% D. 50 - 60%

14. The range of normal metabolism is *generally* considered to be: 14.____

A. minus 5 to plus 5
B. minus 10 to plus 10
C. minus 20, to plus 20
D. minus 25 to plus 25

15. If a patient ate everything served him for breakfast except 10 grams of bacon, his caloric intake for this meal would be decreased by ______ calories. 15.____

A. 10 B. 40 C. 60 D. 90

16. If you were asked to prepare one quart of 1-1000 solution of mercuric chloride from tablets 0.5 grams, *how many* tablets would you use? 16.____

A. 2 B. 5 C. 7 1/2 D. 13

17. The discomfort of constipation is due to 17.____

A. pressure of the fecal material on the rectum
B. absorption of toxins from the colon
C. increased bacterial content in the colon
D. gases produced by the bacillus coli

18. The *one BEST* explanation why soap and water are more effective in cleansing than clear water is that 18.____

A. soap softens the water
B. clear water adheres more closely to the surface of an object
C. the surface tension of a soap-and-water solution is lower than that of clear water
D. clear water promotes absorption

19. In the care of a patient with communicable disease in the home, the *accepted* method for the care of his dishes is: 19.____

A. Wash in the sink
B. Wash in the sink and boil
C. Boil and then wash in the sink
D. Soak in a disinfectant solution and then wash

20. Of the following superficial body areas, the one that would be affected *early* by a diet deficient in niacin is the 20.____

A. cornea B. conjunctiva C. gums D. tongue

21. The *MOST* effective method for cleaning contaminated hands is washing with soap 21.____

A. and hot running water
B. and water in a basin
C. hot running water, and a sterile brush
D. in hot running water, and rinsing in a 70%-solution of alcohol

22. In a *second-degree* burn, the *DEEPEST* tissue affected is the 22.____

A. epidermis
B. dermis
C. subcutaneous tissue
D. muscle

23. The *MOST* desirable first-aid treatment for burns is the use of 23.____

A. tannic acid jelly
B. tannic acid spray
C. vaseline
D. sodium bicarbonate paste

24. An *inexpensive* food source of iron is 24.____

A. potato B. carrots C. milk D. meat

25. One of the substances which is added to "enriched" bread is 25.____

A. Vitamin A B. thiamin C. ascorbic acid D. niacin

KEY (CORRECT ANSWERS)

1. D
2. B
3. B
4. D
5. A

6. D
7. A
8. C
9. B
10. D

11. D
12. C
13. C
14. B
15. B

16. A
17. A
18. C
19. D
20. D

21. D
22. B
23. C
24. A
25. B

COMMON DIAGNOSTIC NORMS

CONTENTS

COMMON DIAGNOSTIC NORMS

1. RESPIRATION: From 16-20 per minute.

2. PULSE-RATE: Men, about 72 per minute.
   Women, about 80 per minute.

3. BLOOD PRESSURE:

Men:	110-135	(Systolic)	Women:	95-125	(Systolic)
	70-85	(Diastolic)		65-70	(Diastolic)

4. BASAL METABOLISM: Represents the body energy expended to maintain respiration, circulation, etc. Normal rate ranges from plus 10 to minus 10.

5. BLOOD:

   a. Red Blood (Erythrocyte) Count:
   Male adult - 5,000,000 per cu. mm.
   Female adult - 4,500,000 per cu. mm.
   (Increased in polycythemia vera, poisoning by carbon monoxide, in chronic pulmonary artery sclerosis, and in concentration of blood by sweating, vomiting, or diarrhea.)
   (Decreased in pernicious anemia, secondary anemia, and hypochronic anemia.)

   b. White Blood (Leukocyte) Count: 6,000 to 8,000 per cu. mm.
   (Increased with muscular exercise, acute infections, intestinal obstruction, coronary thrombosis, leukemias.)
   (Decreased due to injury to source of blood formation and interference in delivery of cells to bloodstream, typhoid, pernicious anemia, arsenic and benzol poisoning.)
   The total leukocyte group is made up of a number of diverse varieties of white blood cells. Not only the total leukocyte count, but also the relative count of the diverse varieties, is an important aid to diagnosis. In normal blood, from:
   70-72% of the leukocytes are *polymorphonuclear neuirophils.*
   2-4% of the leukocytes are *polymorphonuclear eosinophils.*
   0-.5% of the leukocytes are *basophils,*
   20-25% of the leukocytes are *lymphocytes.*
   2-6% of the leukocytes are *monocytes.*

   c. Blood Platelet (Thrombocyte) Count:
   250,000 per cu. mm. Blood platelets are important in blood coagulation.

   d. Hemoglobin Content:
   May normally vary from 85-100%. A 100% hemoglobin content is equivalent to the presence of 15.6 grams of hemoglobin in 100 c.c. of blood.

   e. Color Index:
   Represents the relative amount of hemoglobin contained in a red blood corpuscle compared with that of a normal individual of the patient's age and sex.
   The normal is 1. To determine the color index, the percentage of hemoglobin is divided by the ratio of red cells in the patient's blood to a norm of 5,000,000. Thus, a hemoglobin content of 60% and a red cell count of 4,000,000 (80% of 5,000,000) produces an abnormal color index of .75.

f. Sedimentation Rate:
Represents the measurement of the speed with which red cells settle toward the bottom of a containing vessel. The rate is expressed in millimeters per hour, and indicates the total sedimentation of red blood cells at the end of 60 minutes.

Average rate:	4-7 mm. in 1 hour
Slightly abnormal rate:	8-15 mm. in 1 hour
Moderately abnormal rate:	16-40 mm. in 1 hour
Considerably abnormal rate:	41-80 mm. in 1 hour

(The sedimentation rate is above normal in patients with chronic infections, or in whom there is a disease process involving destruction of tissue, such as coronary thrombosis, etc.)

g. Blood Sugar:
90-120 mg. per 100 c.c. (Normal)
In mild diabetics: 150-300 mg. per 100 c.c.
In severe diabetics: 300-1200 mg. per 100 c.c.

h. Blood Lead:
0.1 mg. or less in 100 c.c. (Normal). Greatly increased in lead poisoning.

i. Non-Protein Nitrogen:
Since the function of the kidneys is to remove from the blood certain of the waste products of cellular activity, any degree of accumulation of these waste products in the blood is a measure of renal malfunction. For testing purposes, the substances chosen for measurement are the nitrogen-containing products of protein combustion, their amounts being estimated in terms of the nitrogen they contain. These substances are urea, uric acid, and creatinine, the sum total of which, in addition to any traces of other waste products, being designated as total non-protein nitrogen (NPN).

The normal limits of NPN in 100 c.c. of blood range from 25-40 mg. Of this total, urea nitrogen normally constitutes 12-15 mg., uric acid 2-4 mg., and creatinine 1-2 mg.

6. URINE:

a. Urine - Lead:
0.08 mg. per liter of urine (normal).
(Increased in lead poisoning.)

b. Sugar:
From none to a faint trace (normal).
From 0.5% upwards (abnormal).
(Increased in diabetes mellitus.)

c. Urea:
Normal excretion ranges from 15-40 grams in 24 hours.
(Increased in fever and toxic states.)

d. Uric Acid:
Normal excretion is variable. (Increased in leukemia and gout.)

e. Albumin:
Normal renal cells allow a trace of albumin to pass into the urine, but this trace is so minute that it cannot be detected by ordinary tests.

f. Casts:
In some abnormal conditions, the kidney tubules become lined with substances which harden and form a mould or *oast* inside the tubes. These are later washed out by the urine, and may be detected microscopically. They are named either from the substance composing them, or from their appearance. Thus, there are pus casts, epithelial casts from the walls of the tubes, hyaline casts formed from coagulable elements of the blood, etc.

g. Pus Cells:
These are found in the urine in cases of nephritis or other inflammatory conditions of the urinary tract.

h. Epithelial Cells:
These are always present in the urine. Their number is greatly multiplied, however, in inflammatory conditions of the urinary tract.

i. Specific Gravity:
This is the ratio between the weight of a given volume of urine to that of the same volume of water. A normal reading ranges from 1.015 to 1.025. A high specific gravity usually occurs in diabetes mellitus. A low specific gravity is associated with a polyuria.

7. SPINAL FLUID:

a. Spinal Fluid Pressure (Manometric Reading):
100-200 mm. of water or 7-15 mm, of mercury (normal).
(Increased in cerebral edema, cerebral hemorrhage, meningitis, certain brain tumors, or if there is some process blocking the fluid circulation in the spinal column, such as a tumor or herniated nucleus pulposus impinging on the spinal canal.)

b. Quickenstedt's Sign:
When the veins in the neck are compressed on one or both sides, there is a rapid rise in the pressure of the cerebrospinal fluid of healthy persons, and this rise quickly disappears when pressure is removed from the neck. But when there is a block of the vertebral canal, the pressure of the cerebrospinal fluid is little or not at all affected by this maneuver.

c. Cerebrospinal Sugar:
50-60 mg. per 100 c.c. of spinal fluid (normal).
(Increased in epidemic encephalitis, diabetes mellitus, and increased intracranial pressure.)
(Decreased in purulent and tuberculous meningitis.)

d. Cerebrospinal Protein:
15-40 mg. per 100 c.c. of spinal fluid (normal).
(Increased in suppurative meningitis, epileptic seizures, cerebrospinal syphilis, anterior poliomyelitis, brain abscess, and brain tumor.)

e. Colloidal Gold Test:
This test is made to determine the presence of cerebrospinal protein.

f. Cerebrospinal Cell Count:
0-10 lymphocytes per cu. mm. (normal).

g. Cerebrospinal Globulin:
Normally negative. It is positive in various types of meningitis, various types of syphilis of the central nervous system, in poliomyelitis, in brain tumor, and in intracranial hemorrhage.

8. SNELLEN CHART FRACTIONS AS SCHEDULE LOSS DETERMINANTS:

a. Visual acuity is expressed by a Snell Fraction, where the numerator represents the distance, in feet, between the subject and the test chart, and the denominator represents the distance, in feet, at which a normal eye could read a type size which the abnormal eye can read only at 20 feet.
b. Thus, 20/20 means that an individual placed 20 feet from the test chart clearly sees the size of type that one with normal vision should see at that distance.
c. 20/60 means that an individual placed 20 feet from the test chart can read only a type size, at a distance of 20 feet, which one of normal vision could read at 60 feet.
d. Reduction of a Snellen Fraction to its simplest form roughly indicates the amount of vision remaining in an eye. Thus, a visual acuity of 20/60 corrected implies a useful vision of 1/3 or 33 1/3%, and a visual loss of 2/3 or 66 2/3% of the eye.

Similarly:

Visual Acuity (Corrected)	Percentage Loss of Use of Eye
20/20	No loss
20/25	20%
20/30	33 1/3%
20/40	50%
20/50	60%
20/60	66 2/3%
20/70	70% (app.)
20/80	75%
20/100	100% (since loss of 80% or more constitutes industrial blindness)

BASIC FUNDAMENTALS OF MEDICATION ADMINISTRATION

CONTENTS

BASIC FUNDAMENTALS OF MEDICATION ADMINISTRATION

I. GUIDELINES FOR MEDICATION ADMINISTRATION

A. General

PURPOSE

To administer the right medication, in the right dose, by the right route, to the right patient, at the right time

PROCEDURE	SPECIAL CONSIDERATIONS
• Transcribe medication and treatment orders from doctor's orders to • Medication and Treatment Cards • Nursing Care Plan • Medication Administration Record (MAR)	Follow local policy.
• Check ALL Medication and Treatment Cards against Nursing Care Plan at the beginning of each shift.	
• Return cards to medication and treatment board, placing each card in space corresponding to hour when medication is due.	
• Clean working area.	
• Wash your hands.	
• Obtain supplies and equipment such as tongue blades, paper cups, pitcher of water, medication tray or cart, and stethoscope.	Keep cards for same patient together.
• Separate cards into • oral medications • injections • treatments	
• Arrange cards in sequence similar to placement of patients on ward.	
•Turn cards face down, turn top card up, and read information on card.	
• Locate medication and compare label on medication with name of medication and dosage on card.	FIRST MEDICATION CHECK.

GUIDELINES FOR MEDICATION ADMINISTRATION, GENERAL (cont)

PROCEDURE	SPECIAL CONSIDERATIONS
• Remove medication container and compare label on container with name of medication and dosage on card.	SECOND CHECK.
• Pour required dosage and compare label on container with card for name of medication and dosage.	THIRD CHECK.
• Place medication and card on tray or cart.	NEVER leave medication cart or tray unattended.
• Continue with remaining cards in same manner.	
• Lock medication cabinet before leaving the area.	
• Administer only medications that you personally prepared.	NEVER allow others to administer medication that you prepared.
• Check name on bed tag with name on card.	FIRST ID CHECK.
• Compare name on card with patient's ID band.	SECOND CHECK.
• Ask patient: "What is your name?" Be sure response is accurate.	THIRD CHECK.
• Administer medication ONLY if all 3 checks agree.	
• Place card face down on one side of tray.	
• Continue to administer medications until all are given.	
• Reset tray or cart for next use.	
• Take cards to desk.	
• Record medications, time and date given, and your initials on MAR using cards as guide.	
• Replace cards on board at next hour due.	

B. *Unit Dose*

PURPOSE

To administer single-dose medication in ready-to-use form

PROCEDURE

- See "Guidelines for Medication Administration, General."
- Get stocked medication cart from storage area.

  Special considerations: Cart is stocked by pharmacy personnel.
- Unlock cart.

  Special considerations: Follow local policy.
- Wheel medication cart to bedside, check MAR, and identify patient.
- Open cassette drawer.
  - Read MAR.
  - Select medication from cassette drawer.
- Check medication against MAR for date, dosage, and route.
- Administer medication and record immediately on MAR.
  - Remain with patient until medication has been taken.
  - Replace drawer in correct space in cassette.
- Dispose of litter, syringe, and needle before moving to next patient.
  - Break off tip of needle and syringe, and dispose in dirty needle box.
  - Place glass unit dose liquid container in bag for return to pharmacy.
- Lock cart and return to storage area.

SPECIAL CONSIDERATIONS

Cart is stocked by pharmacy personnel.

Follow local policy.

II. MEDICATION ADMINISTRATION RECORD (MAR)

PURPOSE

To maintain a permanent record of medication administered

PROCEDURE	SPECIAL CONSIDERATIONS
•Stamp MAR with Addressograph as shown in figure 6-1 on the following page.	
• Enter ward number at bottom right of form; record month and year in space provided at the top.	Make all entries in black ink.
• Transcribe scheduled medications from doctor's orders to front of form.	
• Enter order date, medication dosage, frequency, and route of administration.	
• Complete "Hours" column to indicate scheduled hours for administration starting with earliest military time after 2400 hours.	
• Complete "Dates Given" blocks at top of form.	
• Enter month and dates for a 7day period, starting with first day medication is given.	
• Cancel vacant spaces with an "X."	
• Draw a heavy line across page under last entry and enter next medication directly below.	Do not skip a space.
• When medication has been given, enter your initials in column corresponding to date and hour of administration.	
• Place an "*" in column if the medication was .not given and state reason on Nursing Notes.	
• Place an "L" under date and opposite hour patient is on liberty.	Follow local policy.
• When medication is stopped, bracket remaining spaces for that day; write "STOPPED," enter date and initials.	Applies to scheduled drugs, PRN, and variable dose medications.
• Complete "Initial Code" section.	

NAVMED 6550/8 (REV. 4-74) S/N 0105-LF-...

MEDICAL RECORD

MEDICATION ADMINISTRATION RECORD

SCHEDULED DRUGS

MONTH June 2009 DATES GIVEN

ORDER DATE	MEDICATION-DOSAGE-FREQUENCY ROUTE OF ADMINISTRATION	HOURS	6/19/79	6/20	6/21	6/22	6/23	6/24	6/25
6/19/09	Digoxin 0.25mg PO QD	0800	JLD	*	JLD	JLD	JLD		
	APICAL PULSE →		72	58	64	68	70		
6/19/09	INDERAL 40mg PO Q6H	0600	X	JEP	JEP	STOPPED 6/22/79 JLD			
		1200	X	JLD	JLD				
		1800	JMW	JMW	JMW				
		2400	JMW	JEP	JEP				
6/19/09	Regular Insulin Sliding Scale								
	Glucose 4+ Reg. Insulin 10U sc	0700	JLD 5U	X	JLD 10U	X	JLD 10U		
	Glucose 3+ Reg. Insulin 7U sc	1100	X	X	X	RAB 7U	X		
	Glucose 2+ Reg Insulin 5U sc	1600	JMW 5U	JMW 7U	X	X	X		
	Glucose 1+ Reg. Insulin 0U sc	2100	X	X	X	X	X		
6/19/09	MAALOX 15ml PO Q1H	0700-1500	JLD	JLD	JLD	RAB	JLD		
		1600-2300	JMW	JMW	JMW	JMW	JMW		
		2400-0700	JEP	JEP	JEP	JEP	JEP		
6/20/09	DECADRON (Decreasing dose)	0200	X	RAB 4mg	RAB 3mg	RAB 2mg	SEB 1mg		
	4mg PO Q4H x 12hrs	0600	X	RAB 4mg	RAB 3mg	RAB 2mg	RAB 1mg		
	3mg PO Q4H x 24 hrs	1000	X	RAB 4mg	RAB 3mg	RAB 2mg	RAB 1mg		
	2mg PO Q4H x 24 hrs	1400	X	SEB 3mg	SEB 2mg	SEB 1mg	SEB 0.5mg		
	1mg PO Q4H x 24 hrs	1800	X	SEB 3mg	SEB 2mg	SEB 1mg	SEB 0.5mg		
	0.5mg PO Q4H x 12 hrs then DC	2200	X	SEB 3mg	SEB 2mg	SEB 1mg	SEB 0.5mg		

INITIAL CODE

INITIAL	FULL SIGNATURE & TITLE	INITIAL	FULL SIGNATURE & TITLE	INITIAL	FULL SIGNATURE & TITLE
JLD	John L. Doe LT NC USN				
JMW	Jane M. White LT NC USN				
SEB	Stanley E Baker HM3 USN				
RAB	Ronald A Barnes HN USN				
JEP	Joan E Pierce CDR NC USN				
CFR	Charles F Roberts HM3 USN				

ADDRESSOGRAPH PLATE

J-999999 00-123-45-6789
24JAN79 PROT M E9
22MAY36 MMCM/USN/ACT
DOE, JOHN E. AAA

Injection Site Code

1 - Left Buttock
2 - Right Buttock
3 - Left Deltoid
4 - Right Deltoid
5 - Left Leg
6 - Right Leg
7 - Left Arm
8 - Right Arm
9 - Abdomen

WARD NO T1

SINGLE DOSE PRE OP PRN & VARIABLE DOSE ORDERS SEE REVERSE

Figure 1. Sample Entries on Medication Administration Record (Front).

MEDICATION ADMINISTRATION RECORD (cont)

PROCEDURE

- Transcribe single-order medication, dosage, route of administration, and date and time to be given on back of form. See figure 2 on the following page.

- After administering medication, initial appropriate block.

- Transcribe each preoperative (PREOP) medication dosage, and route of administration on succeeding lines.

- Enter your initials after administering medications.

- Transcribe PRN and variable dose medications from doctor's orders to back of form (fig. 2).

- Enter order date, medication, dosage, frequency, route, and reason for medication.

- Enter date, time, dose, and your initials after administering medication.

NOTE: Some medication orders require modification of basic transcription and charting techniques (fig. 1). These include:

- increasing or decreasing dose medications
- medications requiring apical pulse assessment before administration
- medications administered every other day
- medications such as insulin administered per sliding scale

SPECIAL CONSIDERATIONS

A bracket may be used to show that all PREOP medications are to be given on the same date and time.

For variable dose medications, the dosage need not be the same for each entry.

MEDICATION ADMINISTRATION RECORD (Back) S/N 0105-LF-216-5581

SINGLE ORDERS -- PRE-OPERATIVE

MEDICATION-DOSAGE ROUTE OF ADMINISTRATION	GIVEN DATE	TIME	INITIAL	MEDICATION-DOSAGE ROUTE OF ADMINISTRATION	GIVEN DATE	TIME	INITIAL
Nitroglycerine 0.4 mg Subling.	6/19/09	1200	JLD				
Demerol 100 mg IM } Pre op	6/24/09	0700	JLD				
Nembutal 100 mg IM }	6/24/09	0700	JLD				

PRN AND VARIABLE DOSE MEDICATIONS

ORDER DATE	MEDICATION-DOSAGE FREQUENCY ROUTE OF ADMINISTRATION		DOSES GIVEN
6/22/09	Diazepam 5mg PO PRN restlessness	DATE	6/22
		TIME	1800
		DOSE	5mg
		INIT.	SLB
		DATE	
		TIME	
		DOSE	
		INIT.	

Figure 2. Sample Entries on Medication Administration Record (Back).

III. *DROPS*

A. *Ear*

PURPOSE

To instill medication into the auditory canal

PROCEDURE	SPECIAL CONSIDERATIONS
• See "Guidelines for Medication Administration, General."	Patients should have their own properly labeled medication and it should be at room temperature.
• Position patient on side with affected ear upward.	
• Clean external auditory canal gently with cotton applicators.	Avoid traumatizing when dry-wiping ear canal.
• Straighten auditory canal by gently pulling lobe upward and backward.	

DROPS, EAR (cont)

PROCEDURE

- Instill prescribed number of drops holding dropper nearly horizontally.

SPECIAL CONSIDERATIONS

Support head as needed. Allow medication to fall to side of canal.

- Place cotton loosely in external auditory canal (if ordered).
- Instruct patient to remain in position with treated ear upward for about 5 minutes.

SUPPLIES AND EQUIPMENT

Applicators, cotton tipped

Cotton balls

B. *Eye*

(Ointment Included)

PURPOSE

To apply medication to eye tissue

PROCEDURE

- See "Guidelines for Medication Administration."
- Verify eye to be medicated.
- Tilt patient's head backward and sideways so solution will run away from tear duct.
- Clean eye gently with cotton ball.
- Retract lower lid.
- Instruct patient to look upward.
- Drop medication onto lower lid as shown in figure 3.

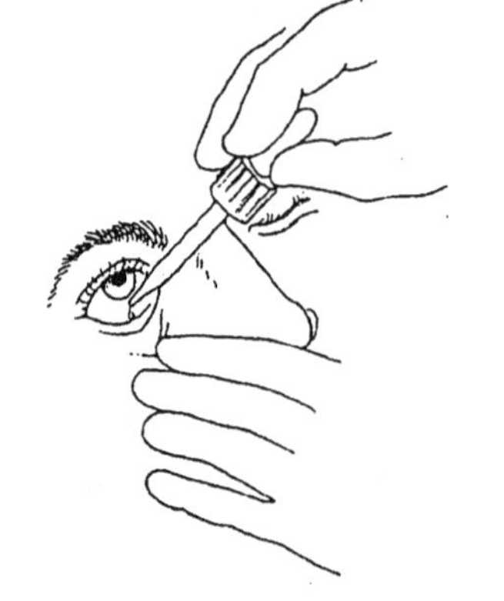

Figure 3. Instilling Eye Drops.

SPECIAL CONSIDERATIONS

If both drops and ointment are ordered, instill drops before applying ointment. Patients should have their own properly labeled medication.

Some solutions are toxic if absorbed through the nose or pharynx.

Do not permit dropper or tip of ointment tube to touch the eye. Avoid contaminating medicine container.

DROPS, EYE (cont)

PROCEDURE

• Apply ointment onto conjunctiva of lower lid as illustrated in figure 4.

• Place dropper in bottle or put cap on ointment tube.

• Instruct patient to close eye.

• Wipe excess medication from inner to outer eye with sterile 2x2s then discard.

SPECIAL CONSIDERATIONS

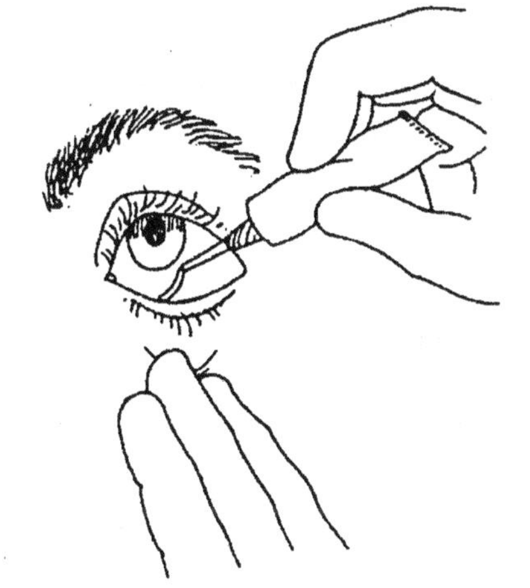

Figure 4. Instilling Eye Ointment.

SUPPLIES AND EQUIPMENT

Cotton balls

Sterile gauze 2x2s

c. *Nose*

PURPOSE

•To instill medication into the nose

PROCEDURE

• See "Guidelines for Medication Administration."

• Tilt patient's head backwards.

• Fill dropper with medication.

• Instill prescribed dosage into nostril as shown in figure 5.

• Place tissues within easy reach.

• Keep patient in position for about 2 minutes.

Figure 5. Instilling Nose Drops.

SPECIAL CONSIDERATIONS

Patients should have their own properly labeled medication.

Do not permit medication to touch rubber bulb of dropper.

Avoid touching nostril with tip of dropper.

IV. GASTRIC TUBES

PURPOSE

To administer medications into the stomach through a tube

PROCEDURE

SPECIAL CONSIDERATIONS

• See "Guidelines for Medication Administration, General:"

• Crush all tablets and add 30 ml tap water.

• Assemble equipment and take to bedside.

• Elevate head of bed unless contraindicated.

Decreases risk of aspiration and regurgitation.

• Expose feeding tube.

• Place protective pad under tubes.

• Check stomach tube for correct placement.

Notify physician if tube is not placed properly.

- Aspirate for gastric contents.
- Listen with stethoscope for air entering stomach as 5 to 10 cc of air is injected into tube.

• Attach irrigating syringe to tube with plunger removed.

• Instill medication into irrigating syringe.

• Follow medication with 30 ml water and allow to flow by gravity.

Ensures patient receives all medication.

• Clamp tube and cover end for 20 to 30 minutes unless contraindicated.

Allows medicine to be absorbed.

• Reattach tube to suction if indicated.

• Rinse and clean;syringe with tap water.

• Return syringe to bedside storage.

• Record amount of water instilled on I&O worksheet.

• Record medication administered on MAR.

GASTRIC TUBES (cont)

SUPPLIES AND EQUIPMENT

Clamp Emesis basin Gauze sponges 4x4

Irrigating syringe, 60 ml Protective pad Rubber band

Sterile dressing (if ordered) Stethoscope Tap water

V. HEPARIN LOCKS

PURPOSE

To administer medications through a heparin lock

PROCEDURE	SPECIAL CONSIDERATIONS
• See "Guidelines for Medication Administration, General."	
• Assemble IV piggyback (IVPB) medication and IV administration set; attach small gauge needle to end of tubing.	
• Fill two 2 1/2 ml syringes with 2 ml normal saline.	
• Withdraw 0.9 ml normal saline and 0.1 ml heparin 1:1000 into a TB syringe.	
• Take equipment to bedside.	
• Determine patency of heparin lock. • Attach first 2 1/2 ml syringe with saline. • Aspirate and observe for blood return. • If no blood returns, check for infiltration by slowly injecting small amount of normal saline. • If infiltrated, remove heparin lock and insert new one.	
• Flush lock with 2 ml normal saline to flush out heparin.	
• Attach IVPB medication infusion set to heparin lock.	
• Administer medication.	Incompatibilities may exist resulting in a precipitate.
• Flush lock with second syringe of normal saline.	

HEPARIN LOCKS (cont)

PROCEDURE	SPECIAL CONSIDERATIONS
• Flush lock with heparin solution.	
• Record medication given on MAR.	

SUPPLIES AND EQUIPMENT

Alcohol sponges Heparin 1:1000	IV administration set IVPB infusion set Needle, 23 ga	Syringes, 2 1/2 ml (2), TB (1)

IV. INJECTIONS

A. *General*

In this section, intramuscular, intradermal, and subcutaneous injections are outlined. Many of the steps are the same for all three methods of injection. Therefore, follow the basic procedure listed below and refer to the specific procedure for special details and equipment.

PROCEDURE	SPECIAL CONSIDERATIONS
•See "Guidelines for Medication Administration, General."	See equipment list of specific procedure.
• Assemble equipment in preparation area. • Remove syringe from sterile pack. • Loosen the plunger by withdrawing once or twice. • Assemble syringe and needle.	
•Tighten needle.	
•Score ampule with file if not prescored.	Prescored ampules are usually indicated by colored ring.
•Clean ampule or vial with antiseptic sponge and break away top of ampule.	
•Discard ampule top and sponge.	
•Remove needle guard and place on counter for reuse.	
• Draw enough air into syringe to equal in volume the dose of medication ordered.	Does not apply to ampules.

INJECTIONS, GENERAL (cont)

PROCEDURE

• Insert needle into medication using aseptic technique. See figure 6.

• Withdraw slightly more medication than required dose.

• Remove needle from ampule or vial.

• Hold syringe and needle vertically.
  • Tap syringe with finger to dislodge air bubbles.
  • Aspirate to clear needle of solution.
  • Push solution up to needle hub.
  • Tip needle and syringe expelling excess solution into sink.
  • Cover and remove used needle.
  • Attach new sterile needle.
  • Read calibrations on syringe barrel at eye level to ensure correct dosage.

• Take syringe and antiseptic sponge to patient's bedside.

• Identify patient.

• Explain procedure to patient.

• Select injection site and position patient accordingly, avoiding undue exposure.

• Clean area with antiseptic sponge.

SPECIAL CONSIDERATIONS

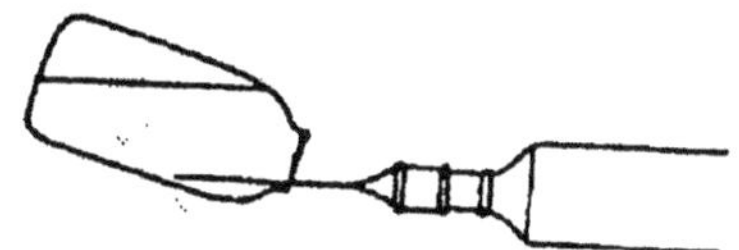

Figure 6. Withdrawing Medication from Ampule.

Figure 6. Withdrawing Medication from Ampule.

Do not allow solution to run down shaft of needle.

REFER TO SPECIFIC PROCEDURE:INTRAMUSCULAR, Z-TRACT,INTRADERMAL,INTRAVE-NOUS, SUBCUTANEOUS, OR INSULIN. After performing specific procedure

• Clip off needle and tip of syringe then discard.

B. *Intramuscular* (IM)

PURPOSE

To administer sterile medications intramuscularly

PROCEDURE

• See "Injections, General."

• Select injection site. See figure 7.

• Position patient.
  • Place on abdomen "toeing in" for gluteal area.
  • Place on side for ventral gluteal area.

• Clean area with antiseptic sponge.

• Hold tissue taut and insert needle at 90° angle as shown in figure 8.

• Aspirate. If blood appears
  • withdraw needle
  • discard medication
  • prepare new dose

• Inject medication slowly.

• Remove needle quickly while holding skin taut.

• Place antiseptic sponge over injection site exerting slight pressure.

SPECIAL CONSIDERATIONS

Preferred site is the ventral gluteal area.

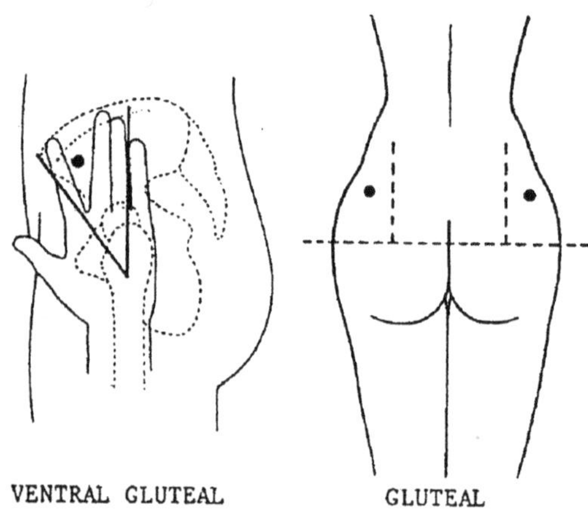

Figure 7. Intramuscular Injection Sites.

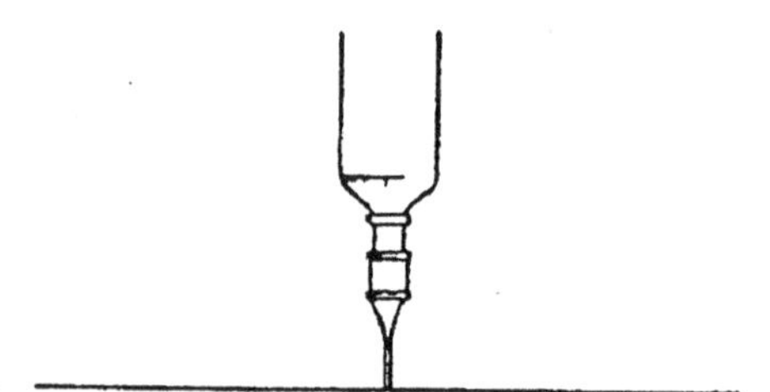

Figure 8. Intramuscular Injection Angle.

SUPPLIES AND EQUIPMENT

Antiseptic sponges (2)

Syringe, 1 to 5 ml

Needle, 21 or 22 ga, 1 1/4 ga

1. Z-Tract

PURPOSE

To prevent backflow of medication from IM injection into subcutaneous tissue

PROCEDURE

- See "Injections, General."
- Position patient.
    - Place on abdomen "toeing in" for gluteal area.
    - Place on back for vastus lateralis area.
    - Place on side for ventral gluteal area.
- Clean area with antiseptic sponge.
- Pull skin downward or to the side and insert the needle proximal to midmuscle mass downward at an oblique angle.
- Insert needle quickly with bevel up.
- Aspirate. If blood appears
    - withdraw needle
    - discard medication
    - prepare new dose
- Inject medication slowly and empty syringe completely.
- Remove needle quickly, holding skin taut.
- Release skin and wipe area with antiseptic sponge.

SPECIAL CONSIDERATIONS

C. *Intradermal* (ID)

PURPOSE

To test for sensitivity to foreign substances

PROCEDURE

- See "Injections, General."
- Select injection site.
- Clean area with antiseptic sponge.

SPECIAL CONSIDERATIONS

Usual dose for ID testing is 0.1 ml or less.

INJECTIONS, ID (cont)

PROCEDURE	SPECIAL CONSIDERATIONS
• Grasp forearm securely on both sides of injection site. • Place thumb on one side and forefinger on the other. • Hold skin taut.	
• Insert needle just under skin surface at a 15° angle with bevel up. See figure 9.	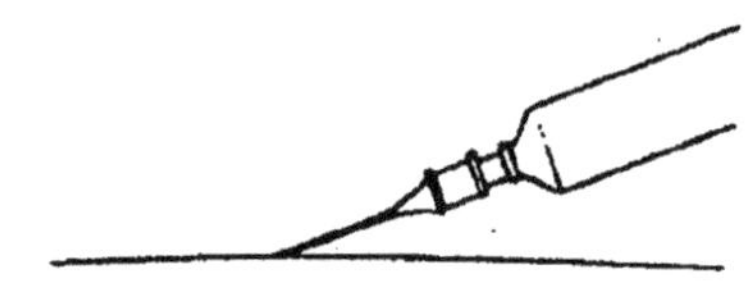 Figure 9. Intradermal Injection Angle.
• Inject solution slowly to produce a bubble or wheal.	
• Remove needle.	Do not massage.
• Read skin test.	Follow local policy.

SUPPLIES AND EQUIPMENT

Antiseptic sponges (2) | Needle, 26 or 27 ga, 1 in | Syringe, TB

D. *Intravenous Piggyback*

(IVPB)

PURPOSE

To administer medications through an IV line

PROCEDURE	SPECIAL CONSIDERATIONS
• See "Guidelines for Medication Administration, General."	
• Units with IV admixture	Pharmacy may prepare fluids with added medications.
• Check for correctness of medication as in guidelines above.	
• Units without IV admixture	
• Prepare medications and draw into syringe. • Obtain secondary IV solution ensuring compatibility with medication. • Inject medication into secondary IV solution.	
• Label solution with • name of medication • dosage • date • time • your initials	Do not cover manufacturer's label.

INJECTIONS, IVPB (cont)

PROCEDURE	SPECIAL CONSIDERATIONS
• Close regulator clamp on IVPB administration set.	
• Insert piercing pin through stopper.	Maintain aseptic technique.
• Attach needle to tubing.	Local policy dictates size of needle.
• Clear air from tubing and needle.	
• Label tubing with • date • time • your initials	Tubing and needle must be changed every 24 hours.
• Take equipment to bedside.	
• Identify patient as in guidelines above.	
• Have secondary IV on standard. • Clean upper Y-junction on primary IV set with alcohol swab.	
• Insert secondary needle into Y.	
• Secure needle with tape.	
• Open clamp on secondary set and adjust rate.	Primary and secondary IVs. run simultaneously. IVPBs may not run unless primary bottle is lower. It is not necessary to adjust flow rate of primary bottle. It will begin again when IVPB is empty.
• Record amount of fluid infused on I&O worksheet.	
•Record medication on MAR.	

SUPPLIES AND EQUIPMENT

Adhesive tape
Alcohol swabs
IV administration set
IV solution (50 to 150 ml)
Label
Needle, 23 to 19 ga

E. *Subcutaneous* (SC)

PURPOSE
To administer medications subcutaneously

PROCEDURE
- See "Injections, General."
- Select injection site. See figure 10.
- Clean area with antiseptic sponge.
- Pinch skin between thumb and forefinger.
- Insert needle at 45° angle with bevel up as shown in figure 11.
- Aspirate. If blood appears
    - withdraw needle
    - discard medication
    - prepare new dose
- Inject medication slowly.
- Withdraw needle quickly.
- Place antiseptic sponge over site and apply gentle pressure.

SPECIAL CONSIDERATIONS

Another acceptable site is the anterior lateral aspect of the thigh.

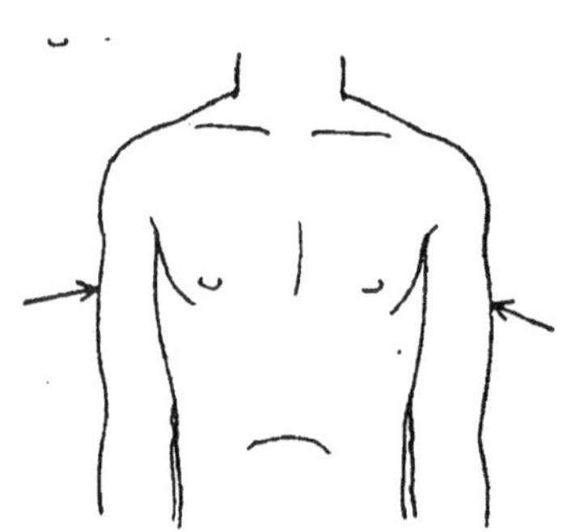

Figure 10. Subcutaneous Injection Site.

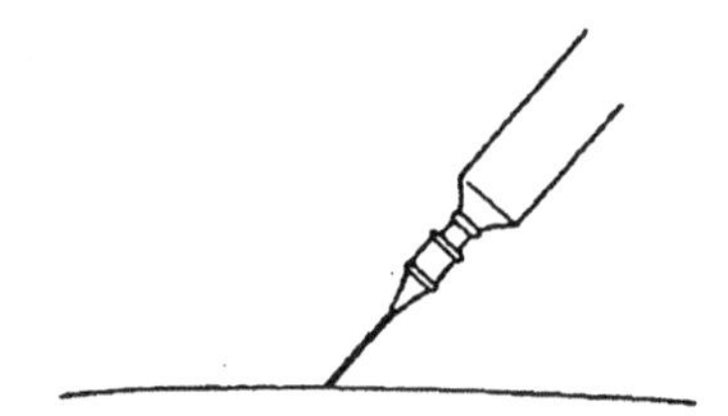

Figure 11. Subcutaneous Injection Angle.

SUPPLIES AND EQUIPMENT

Antiseptic sponges (2)
Needle, 23 ga, 3/4 in
Syringe, 2 1/2 ml

1. Insulin

PURPOSE
To lower blood sugar

PROCEDURE

- See "Injections, General."
- Roll insulin vial between palms to thoroughly mix and warm.

SPECIAL CONSIDERATIONS

INJECTIONS, SC, Insulin (cont)

PROCEDURE

• Have another person (nurse) check dose you prepare.

• Select injection site. See figure 12.
  • Rotate injection sites systematically as directed by local policy.

• Clean area with antiseptic sponge.

• Pinch skin between thumb and forefinger.

• Insert needle at 45° angle with bevel up (fig. ID.

• Aspirate. If blood appears
  • withdraw needle
  • discard medication
  • prepare new dose

• Inject medication slowly.

•Withdraw needle quickly.

•Place antiseptic sponge over site and apply gentle pressure.

SPECIAL CONSIDERATIONS

Do not give to an NPO patient without consulting physician for specific instructions.

Absorption from the arm is more rapid than from the thigh

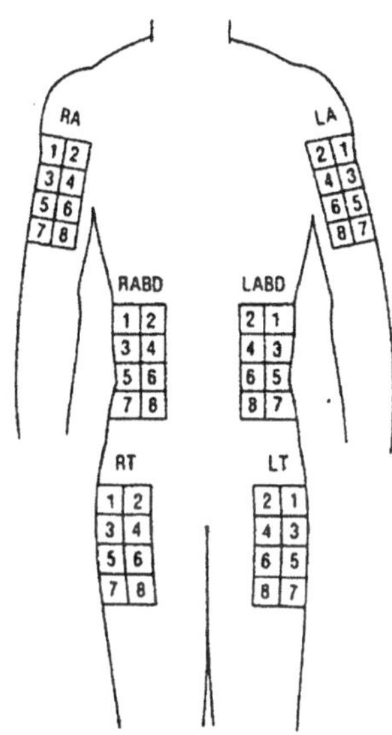

Figure 12. Insulin Injection Sites.

SUPPLIES AND EQUIPMENT

Needle, 23 ga, 3/4 in

Syringe, insulin

VII. ORAL MEDICATIONS

PURPOSE

To prepare and administer medications orally

PROCEDURE

• See "Guidelines for Medication Administration, General."

SPECIAL CONSIDERATIONS

ORAL MEDICATIONS (cont)

PROCEDURE	SPECIAL CONSIDERATIONS
A. Tablets, Pills, or Capsules	
• Instruct patient how to take medication.	For example, if medication is given sublingually, let pill dissolve under toague.
• Check apical pulse rate for 1 full minute before giving cardiotonics. Do not give if rate is below 60 per minute. • Notify nurse or physician. • Record on MAR.	
B. Powders	
• Remove powdered medications from container with a clean, dry, tongue depressor.	
C. Liquids	
• Shake medication if it is a precipitate.	
• Remove bottle , cap and place on counter inside up.	
• Hold bottle with label covered by your palm to prevent soiling label.	
• Measure liquids at eye level using calibrated medication cup.	
• Wipe rim of bottle before recapping.	
• If medication is ordered in drops, count them aloud.	
• Dilute irons, acids, and iodides in 120 ml water and have patient drink through straw. • Irons and iodides stain teeth. •Acids and iodides can irritate mouth.	
•Give cough medications after all others are taken.	Do not dilute or give water following liquid cough medications.

VIII. *SUPPOSITORIES*

A. *Rectal*

PURPOSE

To administer medication rectally

PROCEDURE

- See "Guidelines for Medication Administration, General."
- Screen patient.
- Place patient in left Sim's position.
- Remove protective wrapper from medication.
- Don finger cot or disposable glove.
- Separate buttocks.
- Insert suppository gently through anal opening about 2 inches, using index finger.
- Have patient try to retain suppository for 20 minutes if given to cause bowel movement.
- Hold buttocks together for a minute or two to ensure absorption.
- Remove glove or finger cot and discard.
- Wash your hands.
- Assist patient to a comfortable position as needed.

SPECIAL CONSIDERATIONS

Others can be retained indefinitely.

SUPPLIES AND EQUIPMENT

Finger cot or glove

B. *Urethral*

PURPOSE

To administer medication through the urethra

PROCEDURE

• See "Guidelines for Medication Administration, General."

• Screen patient.

Females

• Place patient on back, legs drawn up and apart, with perineum exposed.

• Remove suppository from wrapper.

• Don disposable glove.

• Separate labia with thumb and forefinger and insert suppository. See figure 13.

• Remove glove and discard.

• Wash your hands.

Males

• Place patient on back with perineum exposed.

• Remove suppository from wrapper.

• Don disposable glove.

• Grasp penis with thumb and forefinger of one hand to expose meatus.

• Insert suppository.

• Remove glove and discard.

• Wash your hands.

SPECIAL CONSIDERATIONS

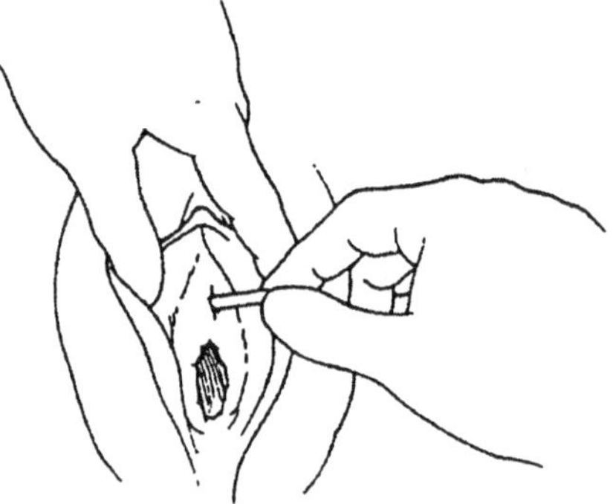

Figure 13. Inserting a Urethral Suppository.

Replace foreskin in uncircum-cised males to prevent constriction.

SUPPLIES AND EQUIPMENT

Glove, disposable

c. Vaginal

PURPOSE

To administer medication vaginally

PROCEDURE.

SPECIAL CONSIDERATIONS

•See "Guidelines for Medication Administration, General."

• Screen patient.

• Position patient in dorsal lithotomy position and expose perineum.

• Remove suppository from wrapper.

• Don disposable glove.

• Separate labia with thumb and forefinger.

• Insert suppository about 2 inches upward and backward into vagina.

• Remove glove and discard.

• Assist patient to comfortable position as needed.

• Wash your hands.

SUPPLIES AND EQUIPMENT

Finger cot or glove

DIAGNOSTIC TESTS AND PROCEDURES

CONTENTS

DIAGNOSTIC TESTS AND PROCEDURES

1. *ABDOMINAL PARACENTESIS*

PURPOSE

To assist the physician in removing fluid from the abdominal cavity and to collect a specimen for diagnostic study

PROCEDURE

- Verify doctor's orders.
- Explain procedure to patient.
- Have patient sign consent form.
- Take and record patient's VS to establish a baseline.
- Give preprocedural medications as ordered.
- Assemble equipment and take to bedside.
- Position patient in high Fowler's position.
- Place protective pad below abdomen.
- Assist physician with draping and anesthetizing patient.
- Observe and report changes in skin color, respirations, and pulse.
- Apply sterile dressing over puncture site and change as ordered.
- Discard disposables.
- Take VS every 15 minutes until stable.
- Label specimen container with patient's ID and send to laboratory with completed request form.

SPECIAL CONSIDERATIONS

ABDOMINAL PARACENTESIS (cont)

PROCEDURE	SPECIAL CONSIDERATIONS
• Check doctor's orders for postprocedural orders.	
• Remove, clean, and store equipment.	
• Record patient's response, amount and description of fluid obtained, and name of physician performing procedure on Nursing Notes.	
• Record date procedure completed on Nursing Care Plan.	

SUPPLIES AND EQUIPMENT

Adhesive tape	Consent form	Needles, Nos. 22 & 25
Antibacterial cleaner	Dry sterile 4x4s	Paracentesis tray
Antiseptic solution	Label for container	Protective pad
Collection basin for fluid	Laboratory request form	Sterile gloves
	Local anesthetic	Syringe, 5 ml

2. BONE MARROW ASPIRATION

PURPOSE

To assist -the physician in obtaining a specimen for diagnostic examination or assessmervt of response to treatment

PROCEDURE	SPECIAL CONSIDERATIONS
• Verity doctor's orders.	
• Explain procedure to patient.	Tell of brief pain caused by aspiration.
• Have patient sign consent form.	
• Take and record patient's VS to establish a baseline.	
• Give preprocedural medications as ordered.	
• Assemble equipment and take to bedside.	
• Assist physician with positioning, preparing, draping, and anesthetizing patient.	Sternum or iliac crest is used.

- Apply pressure to puncture site until bleeding is controlled following procedure.

- Apply dressing

- Have patient lay on iliac crest puncture site for 1 hour to provide pressure.

- Check doctor's orders for postprocedural orders.

- Take VS every 15 minutes until stable.

- Observe frequently every 6 to 8 hours for signs of bleeding and discomfort.

- Label specimen container with patient's ID and send to laboratory with completed request form.

- Discard disposables.

- Remove, clean, and store equipment.

- Record on Nursing Notes:

- name of physician who performed procedure site of puncture

- pertinent observations

- patient's response

- Record date specimen obtained on Nursing Care Plan.

SUPPLIES AND EQUIPMENT

Adhesive tape
Antiseptic skin solution
Bone marrow tray
Consent form
Label for container
Laboratory request form
Local anesthetic
Needles, Nos. 22 & 25
Sodium oxalate or prescribed solution for specimen
Specimen jar/slides
Sterile 4x4s or Band-Aid
Sterile gloves
Syringe, 5 ml

3. CULTURES
A. *Blood*

PURPOSE

To detect the presence of organisms in the blood

PROCEDURE	SPECIAL CONSIDERATIONS
• Verify doctor's orders.	
• Explain procedure to patient.	Follow local policy.
• Assemble equipment and take to bedside.	DO NOT touch prepped area unless gloved; maintain aseptic technique.
• Apply tourniquet and select site.	
• Prep site with antiseptic scrub and allow to dry.	
• Draw 6 to 10 ml blood into sterile syringe.	
• Remove tourniquet.	Prevents accidental entry of air into media.
• Withdraw needle from vein.	
• Apply pressure to site with dry 2x2 gauze.	
• Apply Band-Aid.	
• Remove used needle from blood-filled syringe and attach fresh sterile needle.	
• Innoculate 3 to 5 ml of blood into anerobic vial first. Innoculate remaining blood into aerobic bottle.	
• Label media vials with patient's ID and send to laboratory with completed request form.	
• Discard disposables.	
• Remove, clean, and store equipment.	
• Record date specimen obtained on Nursing Care Plan.	

SUPPLIES AND EQUIPMENT

Antiseptic solution/scrub	Laboratory request form	Tourniquet
Band-Aid	Needle, 21 ga. (2)	2x2s
Blood culture media (anerobic & aerobic)	Syringe, 10 ml	4x4s

B. *Throat*

PURPOSE

To determine the causative organism of some upper respiratory tract infections

PROCEDURE	SPECIAL CONSIDERATIONS
• Verify doctor's orders.	
• Explain procedure to patient.	
• Assemble equipment and take to bedside.	
• Position patient sitting with head tilted back.	
• Hold culture tube in one hand and with the other, remove cap with attached sterile applicator.	Maintain asepsis.
• Have patient open mouth.	
• Depress tongue with tongue blade.	
• Swab pharynx gently with applicator to get a discharge sample.	
• Return applicator to culture tube and cap.	Maintain asepsis of applicator.
• Snap liquid capsule at bottom of culture tube.	Applicator tips should be in contact with the damp cotton in the bottom of the tube.
• Label specimen with patient's ID and send to laboratory with completed request form.	
• Record date specimen obtained on Nursing Care Plan.	

SUPPLIES AND EQUIPMENT

Laboratory request form	Sterile culture tube with cotton tip applicator	Tongue blade

C. *Wound*

PURPOSE

To collect a wound discharge sample for laboratory analysis

PROCEDURE	SPECIAL CONSIDERATIONS
• Verify doctor's orders.	
• Explain procedure to patient.	
• Assemble equipment and take to bedside.	
• Position patient in comfortable position and expose area to be cultured.	
• Hold culture tube in one hand and with the other, remove cap with attached sterile applicators.	Maintain asepsis.
• Swab wound gently to get discharge sample on applicator.	
• Return applicators to culture tube then cap.	Maintain asepsis of applicator.
• Snap liquid capsule at bottom of culture tube.	Applicator tips should be in contact with the damp cotton in the bottom of the tube.
• Redress wound.	
• Discard disposables.	
• Remove, clean, and store equipment.	
• Label specimen with patient's ID and send to laboratory with completed request form.	
• Record date specimen obtained on Nursing Care Plan.	

SUPPLIES AND EQUIPMENT

Adhesive tape
Laboratory request form
Sterile culture tube with cotton tip applicators
Sterile dressing

4. *LIVER BIOPSY*

PURPOSE

To assist the physician in obtaining a sample of liver tissue for diagnostic examination

PROCEDURE	SPECIAL CONSIDERATIONS
• Verify doctor's orders.	
• Explain procedure to patient.	
• Have patient sign consent form	
• Take and record patient's VS to establish a baseline.	
• Give preprocedural medications as ordered.	
• Assemble equipment and take to bedside.	
• Assist with positioning, preparing, draping, and anesthetizing patient.	
• Tell patient to hold breath while physician inserts biopsy needle into liver.	Immobilizes the chest wall and diaphragm decreasing the risk of lacerating the liver.
• Be alert for hypotension, tachycardia, allergic reactions, bleeding, and complaints of pain.	
• Place specimen in container of formaldehyde.	
• Apply dressing.	
• Position patient on right side with pillow under costal margin.	Compression of the liver against the ribs hastens hemostasis of deep tissues and prevents hemorrhage.
• Check doctor's orders for postprocedural orders.	
• Take and record pulse and BP.	
• Label specimen container with patient's ID and send to laboratory with completed request form.	
• Observe and report changes in VS.	Indicates hepatic bleeding or bile peritonitis.

LIVER BIOPSY (cont)

PROCEDURE

- Discard disposables.
- Remove, clean, and store equipment.
- Record pertinent observations and patient's response on Nursing Notes.
- Record date specimen obtained on Nursing Care plan .

SPECIAL CONSIDERATIONS

SUPPLIES AND EQUIPMENT

Adhesive tape
Antiseptic solution
Consent form
Label for container
Laboratory request form

Liver biopsy needle (Meghiui or Silverman)
Liver biopsy set Local anesthetic
Needles, Nos. 22 & 25
Specimen jar with formaldehyde

Sphygmomanome ter
Stethoscope
Sterile gloves (1 pr)
Surgical blade, No. 11
4x4s, sterile (4 pkgs)

5. LUMBAR PUNCTURE

PURPOSE

To assist the physician in obtaining cerebrospinal fluid for diagnostic study, to reduce or measure cerebrospinal pressure, or to administer medications into the spinal cavity

PROCEDURE

- Verify doctor's orders.
- Explain procedure to patient.
- Instruct patient to breathe normally during procedure.
- Have patient sign consent form.
- Take and record patient's VS to establish *a* baseline.
- Ask patient to void.
- Give preprocedural medications as ordered.
- Assemble equipment and take to bedside.

SPECIAL CONSIDERATIONS

Hyperventilation may lower an elevated spinal pressure.

Figure 1. Position for Lumbar Puncture.

LUMBAR PUNCTURE (cont)

PROCEDURE	SPECIAL CONSIDERATIONS
• Position patient in lateral recumbent position (knee-chest) with back at edge of bed to increase space between spinous processes of vertibrae. See figure 1.	
• Place a small pillow under patient's head.	
• Stand on opposite side of physician and assist patient in maintaining position.	
• Assist physician as needed.	
• Label specimens with patient's ID and in sequence; for example, specimen No. 1, specimen No. 2, or specimen No. 3.	
• Apply Band-Aid over puncture site.	
• Check doctor's orders for postprocedural orders.	
• Keep patient on back for 1 to 2 hours unless contraindicated, then allow side-to-side turning.	
• Instruct patient to remain in horizontal position for 12 to 24 hours.	Follow local policy.
• Encourage liberal fluid intake.	
• Take and record VS every 15 minutes until stable, then as ordered.	
• Observe for postpuncture headache.	Due to leaking of cerebrospinal fluid into epidural space.
• Send labeled specimens to laboratory with completed request form.	
• Discard disposables.	
• Remove, clean, and store equipment.	
• Record pertinent observations and patient's response on Nursing Notes.	
• Record date specimen obtained on Nursing Care Plan.	

10

SUPPLIES AND EQUIPMENT

- Antibacterial cleaner
- Antiseptic solution
- Band-Aid
- Consent form
- Gloves, sterile
- Laboratory request form
- Local anesthetic
- Lumbar puncture tray
- Needle, 25 ga
- Specimen label
- Syringe label

6. *SPECIMEN COLLECTION*

A. *Blood*

PURPOSE

To collect a single sample of venous blood through the venipuncture vacuum-assist method

PROCEDURE	SPECIAL CONSIDERATIONS
• Complete laboratory request form.	
• Label specimen container with patient's ID.	
• Select vacuum tube.	
• Affix label to vacuum tube.	
• Assemble needle and holder.	Leave guard on needle.
• Tap tube gently to remove additive around stopper.	
• nsert tube into holder until edge of stopper meets guideline on holder.	If stopper extends beyond guideline, vacuum will be destroyed.
• Take equipment to bedside.	
• Explain procedure to patient.	
• Place protective pad under arm.	Use opposite arm if patient is receiving IV fluids.
• Apply tourniquet about 3 inches above proposed venipuncture site.	Tighten to occlude venous circulation only.
• Cleanse site with antiseptic sponge. • Use circular motion from center out. • Use downward motion to dry wipe.	
• Extend arm downward to prevent backflow from tube to patient. See figure 2.	

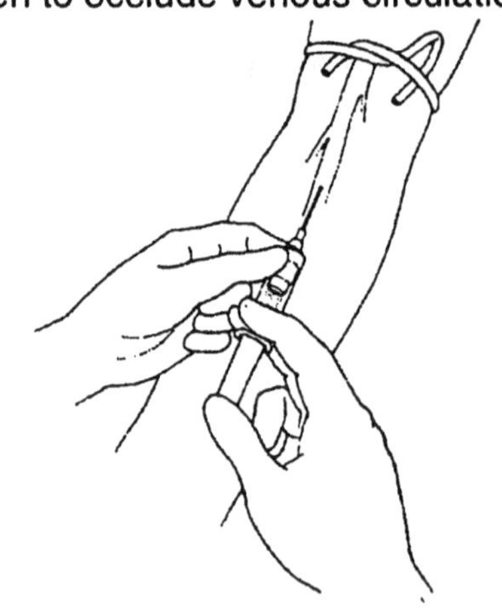

SPECIMEN COLLECTION, BLOOD (cont)

PROCEDURE	SPECIAL CONSIDERATIONS
• Remove needle guard.	
• Ask patient to clench fist to aid in vein distention.	
• Stretch skin downward using thumb to anchor vein about 2 inches below puncture site.	
• Puncture skin and vein with needle bevel up at 15° angle in line with vein.	
• Push tube to bottom of holder.	
• Ask patient to relax fist.	
• Release tourniquet as soon as blood flows into tube.	
• Remove needle from vein after tube is filled. • Apply pressure over insertion site with dry sterile wipe.	Do not permit tube contents to contact stopper or end of needle during procedure. Tube should not fill completely.
• Have patient maintain pressure over site for at least 30 seconds.	
• Elevate arm to prevent bleeding.	
• Remove tube from holder.	
• Invert tube gently to mix additive.	DO NOT SHAKE!
• Attach completed form to specimen and send to laboratory.	
• Discard disposables.	
• Destroy needle.	
• Wash holder in soap and water and return to storage.	
• Record date sample withdrawn on Nursing Care Plan.	

12

Antiseptic wipes	Laboratory request form	Tourniquet
Double-pointed needle	Protective pad	Vacuum tube & holder
	Specimen label	2x2s, sterile

B. Gases

PURPOSE

To measure oxygen, carbon dioxide, and hydrogen in arterial and venous blood

PROCEDURE	SPECIAL CONSIDERATIONS
• Verify doctor's orders.	The laboratory primes the machine.
• Notify laboratory before collecting specimen.	
• Explain procedure to patient.	
• Heparinize syringe and needle by flushing with small amount of heparin.	
• Assist physician in obtaining blood specimen.	
• Cover puncture site with sterile gauze and apply direct pressure for 10 minutes after needle is removed.	
• Tape gauze in place if needed to control bleeding.	
• Observe site in 30 minutes for hemorrhage.	
• If bleeding, notify physician.	
• Expel any air bubbles from syringe and needle.	Air will affect measurement.
• Immediately insert needle tip into but not through a rubber stopper.	Prevents air from entering needle and syringe.
• Place syringe and needle in iced water.	Decreases alteration of true values of O_2, CO_2, and pH.
• Send specimen and completed request form immediately to the laboratory.	Identify origin (arterial or venous) of blood sample.

SPECIMEN COLLECTION, BLOOD GASES (cont)

PROCEDURE

- Discard disposables.
- Remove, clean, and store equipment.
- Record date specimen collected on Nursing Care Plan.

SUPPLIES AND EQUIPMENT

Adhesive tape Alcohol sponges
Cup of iced water

Heparin
Laboratory request form
Rubber stopper (from laboratory specimen tube)

Sterile
Needle
Syringe, 2.5 or 5.0 ml (glass preferred)

C. *Sputum*

PURPOSE

To collect a sputum specimen

PROCEDURE

SPECIAL CONSIDERATIONS

- Verify doctor's orders.
- Explain procedure to patient.
- Assemble equipment and take to bedside.
- Have patient rinse mouth with fresh water.
- Instruct patient to breathe deeply, cough from the chest, and expectorate into sterile specimen container.
- If patient is unable to produce sputum, use mechanical suction, sterile catheter, and sterile sputum trap.
- Label specimen container with patient's ID and send to laboratory with completed request form.
- Discard disposables.

PROCEDURE	SPECIAL CONSIDERATIONS
• Remove, clean, and store equipment.	
• Record date specimen collected on Nursing Care Plan.	

SUPPLIES AND EQUIPMENT

Glass of water	Label for container Laboratory request form	Sterile sputum container

Additional Items When Collecting by Tracheal Aspiration

Sputum trap	Sterile Gloves Suction catheter	Suction apparatus

D. Stool

PURPOSE

To collect a stool specimen

PROCEDURE	SPECIAL CONSIDERATIONS
• Verify doctor's orders.	
• Explain procedure to patient.	
• Assemble equipment and take to bedside.	Maintain aseptic technique for cultures.
• Have patient notify you when ready to use bedpan.	
• Assist patient onto bedpan.	Place bedpan on commode seat or use portable commode.
• Transfer specimen to container with tongue blade. • Place cover on container and label container with patient's ID.	
• Wash and steam bedpan and return it to bedside storage area.	
• Wash hands.	

PROCEDURE	SPECIAL CONSIDERATIONS
• Send to laboratory immediately with completed request form.	Specimen must be fresh when received in laboratory. When testing for parasites, the specimen must be kept warm.
• Record date specimen collected on Nursing Care Plan.	

SUPPLIES AND EQUIPMENT

Bedpan or portable commode	Laboratory request form	Tongue blades Specimen
Label for container	Toilet paper	container

E. Urine
(1) Clean-Catch, Midstream Voided
a. *Female*

PURPOSE

To collect a cleanly voided urine specimen

PROCEDURE	SPECIAL CONSIDERATIONS
• Verify doctor's orders.	First voided specimen of the day preferred; more concentrated and more likely to reveal abnormalities.
• Explain procedure to patient and encourage participation.	
• Assemble equipment and take to bedside.	
• Position bed patient on bedpan or assist to bathroom if ambulatory.	
• Cleanse perineum using 4x4s wet with soap and water.	Use disposable cleansing towels if available.
• Separate labia to reach meatus.	
• Use downward strokes and use 4x4 for 1 stroke only.	
• Remove secretions from mucous folds of vulva and perineum.	
• Rinse area by using 4x4 saturated with sterile water.	Remove all soap solution; residue may change results.
• Have patient start voiding and discard beginnLng urine.	

PROCEDURE	SPECIAL CONSIDERATIONS
• Record specimen collection date on Nursing Care Plan.	
• Collect midstream urine in sterile basin.	
• Provide means for patient to clean self.	
• Assist patient to bed as necessary.	
• Pour specimen into sterile container.	Avoid contact with inside of container and cap.
• Label specimen container with patient's ID and send to laboratory with completed request form.	
• Discard disposables.	
• Remove, steam clean, and store equipment.	

SUPPLIES AND EQUIPMENT

Bedpan
Disposable cleansing towels
Label for container
Laboratory request form
Soap/water
Sterile
  Basin
(Sterile cont)
Specimen container
4x4s
Toilet paper

b. *Male*

PROCEDURE	SPECIAL CONSIDERATIONS
• Verify doctor's orders.	First voided specimen of the day preferred; more concentrated and more likely to reveal abnormalities.
• Explain procedure to patient and encourage participation.	
• Assemble equipment and take to bedside.	
• Position bed patient with penis exposed or assist to bathroom if ambulatory.	
• Lift penis, retract foreskin, and clean glans with 4x4s wet with soap and water.	Use disposable cleansing towels if available.
• Separate and clean meatus.	
• Use downward strokes, and use 4x4 for 1 stroke only.	

PROCEDURE	SPECIAL CONSIDERATIONS
• Remove all secretions around meatus.	
• Rinse area by using 4x4s saturated with sterile water.	
• Have patient start his stream then stop it.	
• Discard beginning urine.	
• Collect midstream urine in sterile container.	Avoid contact with inside of container and cap. Last few drops of urine are NOT collected; prostatic secretions are introduced into urine at end of urinary stream.
• Provide means for patient to clean self.	
• Replace foreskin in uncircumcised males to to prevent constriction.	
• Label specimen container with patient's ID and send to laboratory with completed request form within the hour of collection.	Urine becomes alkaline if left standing at room temperature.
• Discard disposables.	
• Remove, steam clean, and store equipment.	
• Record specimen collection date on Nursing Care Plan.	

SUPPLIES AND EQUIPMENT

Disposable cleansing towels	Soap/water	(Sterile cont)
Label for container	Sterile	4x4 s
Laboratory request form	Specimen container	Urinal

(2) Closed Drainage System

PURPOSE

To collect a urine specimen

PROCEDURE	SPECIAL CONSIDERATIONS
• Verify doctor's orders.	
• Explain procedure to patient.	
• Assemble equipment and take to bedside.	
• Clamp irrigating tubing if patient is receiving bladder irrigations.	Must be clamped for 1 hour before specimen is collected.
• Clamp indwelling catheter between meatus and collection bag.	Drainage system integrity need not be interrupted to obtain a urine specimen.

PROCEDURE

- Place clamp distal to catheter on drainage system.
- Leave clamped for 10 to 15 minutes only.
- Swab the end of the rubber catheter with an alcohol sponge.
- Insert needle into catheter at angle as shown in figure 3 to avoid going through the catheter.
- Aspirate volume of urine needed for specimen being careful not to deflate the balloon.
- Release clamp on drainage system.
- Unclamp irrigating solution and adjust rate as ordered.
- Transfer urine to specimen container.
- Label specimen container with patient's ID and send to laboratory with completed request form.
- Discard disposables.
- Remove, clean, and store equipment.
- Record volume of urine obtained on I&O worksheet, if applicable.
- Record specimen collection date on Nursing Care Plan.

SPECIAL CONSIDERATIONS

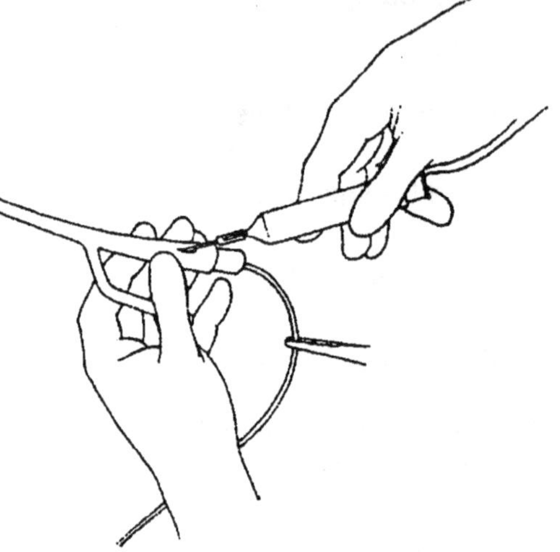

Figure 3. Location and Angle of Needle Insertion

SUPPLIES AND EQUIPMENT

Alcohol sponge
Clamp for catheter
Label for container
Laboratory request form
Needle, 22 ga
Specimen container
Syringe, 10 ml

(3) Twenty-Four Hour

PURPOSE

To collect the total amount of urine excreted in 24 hours

PROCEDURE	SPECIAL CONSIDERATIONS
• Verify doctor's orders.	
• Explain procedure to patient.	
• Take completed request form to laboratory to get a collection container.	Laboratory must have form to ensure proper preservatives are added to container. Form is returned with container.
• Label container with patient's ID.	
• Assemble equipment and take to bedside.	
• Explain dietary and medication restrictions.	Consult local laboratory manual.
• Have patient void and discard urine.	
• Record time of voiding.	Twenty-four hour period begins at this time.
• Provide means for patient to clean self.	Assist as needed.
• Instruct patient to void into bedpan or urinal for next 24 hours.	
• Transfer urine to collection container after each voiding.	
• Store container in cool, dark place.	May require refrigeration. Consult local laboratory manual.
• At end of 24-hour period, have patient void last sample.	Ensure *a* full 24-hour specimen is collected.
• Send specimen container to laboratory with completed request form.	
• Resume preprocedure diet and medications.	
• Record specimen collection date on Nursing Care Plan.	

SUPPLIES AND EQUIPMENT

Bedpan or urinal

Label for container
Laboratory request form

Specimen container

7. Thoracentesis

PURPOSE

To assist the physician in removing fluid and air from the pleural cavity and to collect a specimen for diagnostic study

PROCEDURE	SPECIAL CONSIDERATIONS
• Verify doctor's orders.	Usually pre- and postprocedure chest X-rays are ordered.
• Explain procedure to patient.	
• Have patient sign consent form.	
• Give preprocedural medications.	
• Take and record patient's VS to establish a baseline.	
• Assemble equipment and take to bedside.	
• Assist physician with positioning, preparing, draping, and anesthetizing patient.	Upright position facilitates removal of fluid.
• Apply pressure over puncture site.	
• Apply small sterile dressing over puncture site.	
• Check doctor's orders for postprocedural orders.	
• Turn patient onto unaffected side for about 1 hour.	Allows pleural puncture site to seal itself.
• Take VS every 15 minutes until stable, then as ordered.	Follow local policy.
• Observe and report • faintness • vertigo • tightness in chest • cough • blood-tinged, frothy mucus	Pneumothorax, tension pneumo-thorax, subcutaneous emphysema, pyogenic infection, and pulmonary edema may result from thoracentesis.
• Measure and record amount, color, and consistency of fluid obtained on I&O worksheet.	
• Label specimen with patient's ID and send to laboratory with completed request form.	
• Discard disposables.	

PROCEDURE | SPECIAL CONSIDERATIONS

- Remove, clean, and store equipment.

- Record on Nursing Notes
- name of physician performing procedure
- puncture site
- pertinent observations
- patient's response

•Record date procedure completed on Nursing Care Plan.

SUPPLIES AND EQUIPMENT

Antibacterial cleaner	Local anesthetic	(Sterile cont)
Antiseptic solution/scrub	Needles, Nos. 23 & 25	4x4 s
Consent form	Sterile	Syringes, 5 & 10 ml
Laboratory request form	Gloves	Thoracentesis tray
		Waterproof tape

8. *URINE TESTING*

A. Specific Gravity

PURPOSE

To measure the density of particles in urine to determine the kidneys' diluting and concentrating power

PROCEDURE | SPECIAL CONSIDERATIONS

•Verify doctor's orders.

•Collect fresh urine specimen.

• Pour urine into specific gravity cylinder.

• Float urinometer in specimen. — Do not allow urinometer to touch bottom of cylinder.

• Read lowest point of surface of urine on urinometer.

• Empty cylinder and rinse equipment with clean water.

•Discard specimen and container.

• Record reading on local flowsheet.

• Fresh urine specimen

SUPPLIES AND EQUIPMENT

Fresh urine specimen

Special glass cylinder
Specimen container

Urinometer,

B. Multiple Tests with Reagent Strips

PURPOSE

To analyze the contents of freshly voided urine

PROCEDURE	SPECIAL CONSIDERATIONS
• Verify doctor's orders.	
• Take fresh specimen to utility room.	
• Take reagent strip from bottle without touching test area.	Keep tightly capped as ANY moisture alters test results. Touching alters test results.
• Dip reagent strip in urine.	
• Compare strip with color chart on test strip bottle for results.	Follow directions on bottle for reading time.
• Record results on local flowsheet.	

SUPPLIES AND EQUIPMENT

Color charts

Directions
Specimen cup

Test strips

C. Reagent Tests for Sugar and Acetone

PURPOSE

To test for sugar and acetone in the urine

PROCEDURE	SPECIAL CONSIDERATIONS
• Verify doctor's orders.	Most reliable test results are obtained with double-voided specimens.
• Have patient void and discard urine.	
• Encourage patient to drink several glasses of liquid.	
• Get second specimen 30 to 45 minutes later.	
• Take specimen to utility room.	

Clinitest

SPECIAL CONSIDERATIONS

- Place 5 drops of urine in clean test tube.
- Add 10 drops of water.
- Place test tube in holder.
- Drop 1 Clinitest tablet into test tube.

Do not touch with fingers.

- Wait 15 seconds after boiling stops. Gently shake tube.
- Compare results with Clinitest color chart.
- Notify nurse of abnormal results.
- Remove, clean, and store equipment.

Keep cap of bottle of Clinitest tablets tightly closed to prevent decomposition.

- Record results on local flowsheet.

Acetest

- Place 1 Acetest reagent tablet on paper towel or filter paper.
- Drop 1 or 2 drops of urine on tablet.
- Wait 30 seconds.
- Compare results with Acetest color chart.
- Remove, clean, and store equipment.
- Notify nurse of abnormal results.
- Record results on local flowsheet.

SUPPLIES AND EQUIPMENT

Bedpan or urinal
Color chart
Filter paper
Medicine dropper
Reagent tablet
Specimen cup
Test tube

BASIC FUNDAMENTALS OF MICROBIOLOGY, STERILIZATION, DISINFECTION, AND ASEPTIC TECHNIQUE

CONTENTS

BASIC FUNDAMENTALS OF MICROBIOLOGY, STERILIZATION, DISINFECTION, AND ASEPTIC TECHNIQUE

SECTION A—MICROBIOLOGY

1. Introduction. The activities so often associated with operating room scenes have a very definite purpose. It took a long time for man to understand the cause of infection and to develop methods for preventing it. The science which evolved about the subject is called "microbiology." Microbiology is the study of living things which are of microscopic size. These microorganisms include bacteria, viruses, fungi (molds and yeasts), and animal parasites (worms and protozoa). A knowledge of the basic principles of microbiology is necessary for a clear understanding of the environmental activities carried out in the operating suite.

2. Identification and Classification of Microorganisms. Microorganisms are minute, living structures that are categorized as plants, animals, or viruses. Bacteria are one-celled plants which differ from animal cells. The plant cell has a cell wall made of cellulose in addition to a cell membrane. However, many aspects of plant cells are similar to those of animal cells. These similarities include the facts that both plant and animal cells contain a nucleus and cytoplasm, and both have certain oxygen, temperature, moisture, nutritional, and pH (acid-base) requirements.

a. A few organisms, because of their oxygen requirements, are of special concern to operating room personnel. The oxygen requirement is important because some organisms (aerobes) must have free oxygen to survive. On the other hand, anaerobes, such as those causing tetanus and gas gangrene, can only reproduce in the absence of free oxygen. Anaerobic organisms require special consideration in surgery where deep wounds offer an ideal environment for them to grow and to excrete disease-producing toxins.

b. Not all microorganisms are pathogenic (disease-producing). There are microbes on the skin, in the mouth and nose, in the air, and on practically every object we touch. Most of these never produce disease, and many of them have useful functions in the body, as well as in the world at large. In addition, there are certain organisms which will produce disease only after they are introduced into a particular type of environment. For example, *Escherichia coli*, whose normal habitat is inside the intestine, will produce peritonitis if it ruptures through the intestinal wall. The body defenses, such as white blood cells and certain elements of plasma, fight against the invasion of foreign substances, including microorganisms, and as long as the body remains healthy, many organisms are powerless against these defenses. Once the defenses are broken down as the result of an open wound or because of a generally lowered resistance following surgery, the stage may be set for the entrance and growth of pathogenic organisms, as well as those that would ordinarily never cause any harm.

3. Spore-Forming Bacteria. Certain bacteria (*Bacillus*, for example) are capable of protecting themselves against adverse conditions by the formation of spores. Spores are round granules, which are dry and thick-walled. These granules seem to contain protoplasm in a dehydrated form. Protoplasm is the essential form of matter in which life is manifested. Bacterial spores are the most resistant form of microbial life, and they are far more capable of resisting external destructive agents and of withstanding exposure to temperature extremes than are vegetative cells. Once formed within the bacterial cell, the spore remains dormant until proper growth conditions cause it to germinate into a vegetative cell. Since this dormant period may last for years, viable spores are disseminated so widely in nature that we must assume they are present in most situations involving disinfection and sterilization in medical facilities.

4. Environmental Temperature. The lowest temperature at which a cell will grow is the "minimum temperature," while the highest temperature at which it will grow is the "maximum temperature." "Optimum temperature" is the temperature best suited for a particular organism. The "thermal death point" is that temperature which, in time, will kill all organisms present. Cells will grow and reproduce if an adequate temperature and other needs (oxygen, food, moisture, and pH) are met. ALTERING THE ENVIRONMENTAL CONDITIONS MAY DESTROY OR INHIBIT BACTERIAL GROWTH. THIS FORMS THE BASIS OF ALL SURGICAL ASEPSIS.

5. Bacterial Cultures. Bacterial cells are collected by swabbing a suspect area, using Rodac plates or collecting air samples on culture plates. Sterile, moist swabs must be used if an area is to be swabbed. The cells are then transferred to a tube of culture media or streaked on a culture plate. The tubes or plates are then incubated until the cells reproduce and form colonies which are visible to the naked eye. At this point, they also exhibit clues to the bacteriologist as to their identity. These clues are usually in the form of color, size, and shape. It is from these colonies that the bacteriologist takes samples and sets up slides that finally make microscopic identification possible.

SECTION B—STERILIZATION

6. Introduction. Since the basis for the living process in microorganisms is protein in nature, conditions that adversely affect protein will destroy these cells. Heat, chemical agents, and radiation applied in the proper manner will kill or inhibit the growth of microorganisms. The mechanisms responsible for the destruction of microorganisms are the coagulation of the protoplasmic mass or the chemical alteration of the structure of the cell. THE PROCESS WHICH DESTROYS ALL MICROORGANISMS IS CALLED STERILIZATION.

7. Methods of Sterilization. Operating room personnel should be thoroughly familiar with the various methods of sterilization. Not only should they know how to operate the sterilizing equipment, but they should also be able to select the one most effective in a given situation.

a. Steam under pressure is the most common form of sterilization used in the surgical suite. Microorganisms are destroyed by heat. However, moist heat kills bacteria faster and at a lower temperature than does dry heat. Moisture is provided by steam, and the pressure is used to assure that the steam will attain and maintain the temperature needed for sterilization. In order for the steam under pressure to produce sterility there must be direct steam contact with the item to be sterilized. Anhydrous oils, greases, and powders cannot be sterilized by steam under pressure as the steam cannot penetrate these materials. Otherwise, any item which is not heat or moisture sensitive can be sterilized in a steam-under-pressure sterilizer.

b. Dry heat (hot-air) is another method of utilizing heat for sterilization. The theory is that heat is absorbed from the surface of the substance which is being sterilized. As explained above, dry heat sterilization requires higher temperature and longer exposure time than moist heat. Hot-air sterilizers are impractical for operating room use; therefore, they are seldom available in surgical suites.

c. Gas sterilization is essentially sterilization with a chemical agent. Ethylene oxide, and other gases, are believed to interfere with the chemical make-up of microorganisms, thus rendering them incapable of biological activities. Ethylene oxide gas is used to sterilize heat-labile and moisture-sensitive materials. In addition to the time and temperature factors, gas concentration and controlled moisture also are important in ethylene oxide sterilization. Barriers to gas permeation or diffusion can create problems in attaining sterility.

d. Sterilization by radiation, while not used in hospitals, is commonly used by manufacturers to sterilize many of the prepackaged, presterilized articles used in the operating room.

8. Steam Under Pressure Sterilizers. These sterilizers are designed to hold items for sterilization and to allow steam under pressure to contact or penetrate these items. Figure 1 illustrates the basic design of a steam under pressure sterilizer. There are several types of steam sterilizers and those most widely used are discussed below.

a. *The Downward Displacement Steam Sterilizer.* After the door is closed, steam is admitted through the inlet. Since air is heavier than steam, gravity draws the air downward and outward as steam enters the chamber. This process is rapid when the sterilizer is empty, but when it is filled, air may be trapped in and around the packages causing cool air pockets which prevent the steam from contacting all portions of the contents. Once the steam has displaced the air, the outlet is closed by a heat-sensitive valve activated by the heated steam. After time is allowed for steam to penetrate to the center of linen packs, a specified time is required for sterilization. A thermometer recording system indicates and records the same temperature as that of the thermometer located at the discharge line. It records the length of each exposure cycle over a 24-hour period. The recording chart should be checked at frequent intervals to assure that the correct time and temperatures are being reached and maintained. An automatic timer gives a light or sound signal at the completion of the sterilization cycle. The steam is then exhausted from the chamber and the material is dried before being removed from the sterilizer.

b. *The Prevacuum, High-Temperature Steam Sterilizer.* This sterilizer was designed to provide a faster and more reliable method of sterilization than provided by the downward displacement steam sterilizer. Air trapped inside the sterilizing chamber is one of the greatest dangers encountered in steam-

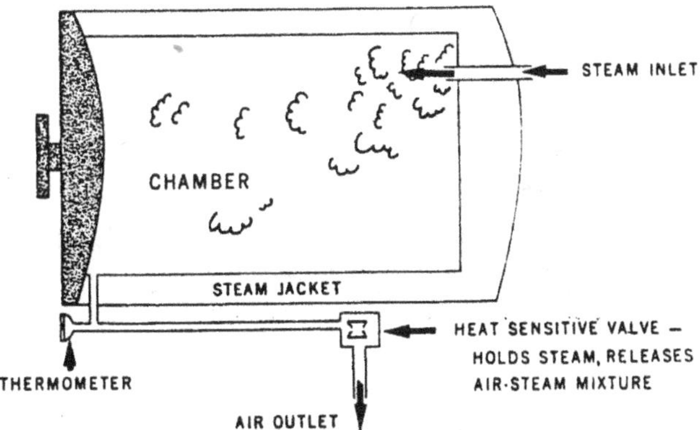

Figure 1. Steam Under Pressure Sterilizer.

under-pressure sterilization. The efficiency of the steam sterilizer is improved by pumping the air from the chamber and creating a nearly perfect vacuum before introducing steam into the chamber. This procedure allows fast and more positive steam penetration of the entire sterilizer load. The cycles of this sterilizer are relatively short due to the fact that the system removes air from the chamber with a vacuum pump and operates at temperatures of 272° F to 276° F. The sterilizing time required is shorter because of prevacuum and higher temperature. The drying time is shorter because of vacuum drying.

c. *The High-Speed, Pressure-Instrument Sterilizer (Flash Sterilizer).* This sterilizer is designed to sterilize surgical instruments. Moist heat, produced by steam under pressure, is the sterilizing agent. Unwrapped instruments which have been dropped or have been omitted from the instrument setup can be sterilized in 3 minutes in a perforated tray. For instruments in a lightly covered or padded tray, the sterilizing time is 10 minutes. Wrapped instruments require 15 minutes for sterilization as extra time is required for the steam to penetrate the fabric and for drying the wrapped packages. However, some flash sterilizers are not equipped with a vacuum dryer. Obviously, wrapped instruments cannot be sterilized in sterilizers which have no drying phase capability. If doubt exists, check the manufacturer's instructions.

d. *Instrument Washer-Sterilizer.* An instrument washer-sterilizer is a pressure vessel which automatically washes, sterilizes, and dries surgical instruments. An agitated detergent bath, which is heated by steam jets, performs the washing. Residual heat in the instruments dries any moisture which remains after the steam is exhausted. The sterilizing cycle of this sterilizer will sterilize clean, unwrapped instruments in 3 minutes. Instruments with other materials, such as suture or rubber tubing, can be sterilized in 10 minutes. This sterilizer is not suitable for sterilizing wrapped instruments as it has no drying capability.

e. *Specific Details.* Specific details for operating these sterilizers have not been included here as their operation may vary according to the manufacturer. Local operating procedures and manufacturer's instructions should be consulted for operating details.

9. Ethylene Oxide Gas Sterilization. Sterilization with ethylene oxide gas is used for articles which would be damaged by the heat or moisture in steam-under-pressure sterilizers. Gas sterilization should not be used for any article which can be steam sterilized.

a. Ethylene oxide is a colorless gas which acts as a vesicant if it comes in contact with the skin. The vapor may cause eye and nose irritation, and overexposure can lead to nausea, vomiting, and dizziness. It is highly flammable and when mixed with air can be ignited by electric spark, static electricity, open flame, or other heat- or spark-producing conditions.

b. To overcome the toxic and flammable properties of ethylene oxide gas, it is mixed with an inert gas, such as carbon dioxide or fluorinated hydrocarbons. These mixtures are relatively safe when correctly used in properly constructed sterilizers.

c. Gas sterilizers look similar to steam sterilizers, but the conditions which produce sterility depend on the concentration of gas and humidity as well as time and temperature. Air is withdrawn from the chamber, and gas is forced in under pressure. The temperature and humidity are then brought to specified levels and held constant for the duration of the sterilizing period. Gas sterilizers must be operated by skilled personnel strictly in accordance with the instructions provided by the manufacturer.

d. Residual ethylene oxide and its byproducts, ethylene glycol and ethylene chlorhydrin, are toxic substances which can remain with articles sterilized by ethylene oxide gas. For this reason, adequate aeration time must be allowed following sterilization to reduce these residuals to a safe level. Aeration may be accomplished in a well-ventilated room. However, a faster and more efficient method is to have specially designed aeration cabinets which provide systematic air changes. Aeration time will be influenced by the type of material as well as the bulk and permeability of the items.

e. Following the manufacturer's instructions is extremely important in the overall process of ethylene oxide sterilization. A copy of the operating instructions should be affixed to each sterilizer and referred to prior to operating the sterilizer and aerating the material. In addition, manufacturer's instructions regarding resterilization of commercially prepared items must be adhered to; for example, articles containing polyvinylchloride which have

A

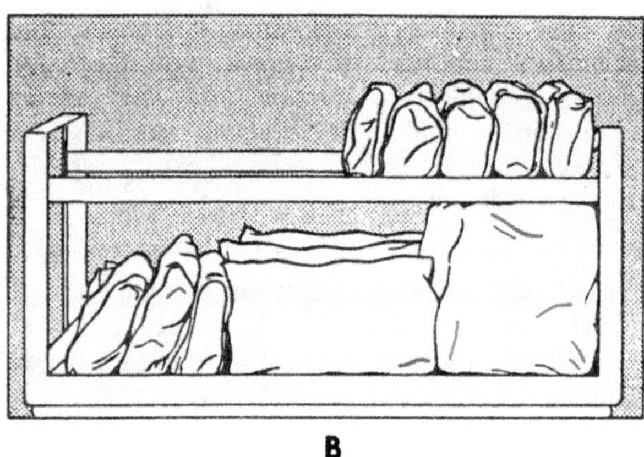

B

Figure 2. Loading Linen Packs and Packages.

been sterilized by gamma radiation must not be resterilized with ethylene oxide as it causes a chemical reaction which produces polychlorhydrin. Polychlordydrin causes toxic reactions to body tissues.

10. Loading the Sterilizer. The integrity of sterilization relies to a great extent on the correct loading of the sterilizer. The steam or gas must be allowed to flow in, around, and out of the articles or packages being sterilized.

a. Packs must be loosely wrapped and not exceed 12 by 12 by 20 inches and 12 pounds in weight.

b. The load should be arranged with the least possible resistance to the free passage of air from all areas of the chamber.

c. The sterilizer must not be overloaded or crowded. The passage of steam or gas from the top to the bottom and around the sides of the chamber must not be blocked.

d. Place all packages on edge, with large linen packs at the bottom and small packages in an upper layer crosswise to the lower layer, as illustrated in figure 2.

e. Utensils (such as pans and basin sets) should be arranged on their sides or edges in positions which allow the air to "spill" out.

f. Articles which require the same type of sterilization (gas or steam) and the same time and temperature may be sterilized together.

g. Fluids must be sterilized separately using slow vacuum to release the steam as high vacuum will pull liquids out of their containers. In vacuum sterilizers, the load is not vacuumed after the exposure time.

11. Errors in Sterilization. Usually errors which cause sterilization failures originate with people. Those errors of primary importance are:

a. Failure to observe and understand the regulation of the sterilizer so that saturated steam is maintained at sterilizing temperature.

b. Incorrect methods of packaging and wrapping supplies.

c. Carelessness in loading the sterilizer, including disregard for the necessity of providing for complete air removal and for free penetration of steam throughout the load.

d. Failure to time the exposure period correctly.

e. Removing wrapped supplies from the sterilizer while they are wet.

f. Equipment which is faulty because it has not been inspected regularly and maintained properly.

12. Sterilization Indicators. There are several ways to keep a constant check on the proper functioning of the sterilizer and to ensure efficient sterilization. Mechanical controls are used to regulate physical conditions in the sterilizer, while the thermal and biological controls test the efficiency within the load that is being processed.

a. Mechanical indicators are devices which are used to assist in identifying and preventing malfunctions and operational errors in the sterilizer.

(1) Indicating thermometers measure the temperature in the sterilizer discharge line throughout the sterilizing cycle. They indicate the temperature on a dial on the face of the sterilizer. It does not detect cool air pockets at the center of the load or linen packs.

(2) Recording thermometers indicate and record the same temperatures that indicating thermometers show. They also record the duration of the exposure time for each sterilizing cycle. If exposure periods are greater or less than prescribed, or if the temperature has not been maintained within proper limits, there is a positive record of the errors, thus providing necessary information upon which to act

in correcting discrepancies. The records of the recorder should contain the number of the sterilizer, the time, and the date. Recording thermometers, like indicating thermometers, do not detect cool air pockets.

b. Thermal indicators are used to detect conditions inside the sterilizer chamber. They are useful for checking packaging and loading techniques as well as exposure to sterilizing cycles. THERMAL INDICATORS DETECT OPERATOR MISTAKES AND/OR STERILIZER MALFUNCTION BUT THEY DO NOT "PROVE" STERILIZATION. The two most widely used types of thermal indicators are:

(1) Heat-sensitive tape that has lines or squares that turn dark when the package is exposed to heat and certain conditions of time and temperature are met. This tape is not a check on the sterility of the package. Its primary function is to indicate that the package has been exposed to a sterilizing cycle.

(2) A sealed glass tube containing a small tablet which melts when certain conditions of heat and temperature are met and maintained for a specified period of time. These tubes are placed at the center of packages as they are wrapped. If the tablet has not melted when the package is opened, then the package has not been exposed to sterilizing conditions.

c. The Bowie-Dick test measures the adequacy of residual air removal and the uniformity of steam penetration in the prevacuum, high-temperature sterilizer. Commercial test sheets or a piece of fabric with 4 or 5, 8-inch strips of heat-sensitive tape crisscrossed on the surface, may be used for the test. The test must be performed daily:

(1) Place the test sheet or fabric in the center of a linen pack and process this single pack through the sterilizing cycle.

(2) Remove the test sheet or fabric from the pack and examine the markings for color change. If the color change is uniform (all lines or circles darkened) it suggests that the sterilizer is functioning properly.

(3) Irregular color changes suggest the presence of residual air in and faulty operation of the sterilizer.

(4) If the prevacuum, high-temperature sterilizer cannot pass the Bowie-Dick test, it should be considered a gravity displacement sterilizer and operated as such.

d. Biological indicators are used to check sterilization efficiency. Negative reports from biological controls prove that wrapping techniques are correct and that the sterilizer is working properly for the load that is being tested. Tests should be conducted once a week, but more frequent testing may be necessary under adverse conditions or when sterilizers are old or troublesome. Commercially prepared spore strips using highly resistant spores in known populations are used to check sterilizer efficiency. Spore strips containing *B. subtilis* are used to check ethylene oxide sterilizers and *B. stearothermophilus* is the organism of choice to check steam sterilizers:

(1) In checking the steam sterilizer, the spore strips are placed in the center of a large linen pack, which is then placed in the front, bottom position of the sterilizer (the position most likely to retain trapped air).

(2) In checking the ethylene oxide sterilizer, the spore strips are placed in various areas throughout the load as well as inside of packaged items.

(3) Following exposure to the sterilizing cycle, the spore strips are sent to a bacteriology laboratory for determination of results. If a bacteriology laboratory is not available locally, the spore strips may be sent to a commercial laboratory or to the manufacturer of the spore strips.

e. If any of the foregoing indicators shows erratic sterilizer operation, trained maintenance personnel should check the sterilizer at once.

13. Steam Sterilizer Maintenance. In order to keep these sterilizers in proper working order, they must be cleaned and inspected regularly. Daily and weekly routines should be established as follows:

a. The interior of the chamber and the chamber drain strainer should be cleaned daily. This cleaning should be done in the morning when the sterilizer is cool:

(1) Wash the inside of the chamber, the door, and all trays, carriages, and racks with a mild detergent and rinse well with plain water. Strong abrasives, steel wool, or similar substances must not be used as they can damage surface areas.

(2) Remove the chamber drain strainer and use a brush to clean lint and sediment from its pores. If the strainer is not kept clean, the sterilizer cannot be depended upon for sterilization.

b. The chamber discharge line and trap should be flushed once a week. Remove the strainer and flush the chamber drain line with a hot solution consisting of 1 ounce of trisodium phosphate to 1 quart of water or use a nonphosphate detergent as a flushing agent. Then flush the line with 1 quart of plain hot water and replace the strainer.

c. Qualified maintenance personnel should inspect and maintain the sterilizers regularly to protect them from superheated (unsaturated) steam, incomplete air exhaustion, and other factors resulting from mechanical failure.

SECTION C—PROCESSING SUPPLIES FOR STERILIZATION

14. Introduction. Specific items which are processed and sterilized in the surgical suite will be determined by local policies, the surgical specialties available, and the extent to which disposable products are used. These items will usually include, but are not limited to, instruments and instrument sets, utensils, linens, and fluids.

15. Cleaning, Sorting, and Inspecting. Instruments, utensils, and similar items must be thoroughly cleaned prior to being processed for sterilization. All foreign material must be removed in order for the sterilizing agent to come in direct contact with the surfaces of the object to be sterilized. For linens the "cleaning" is done by laundering and is accomplished through linen supply. Following thorough cleaning and drying, all items must be sorted, inspected, and tested. Like items should be placed together.

a. Inspect all metal items for signs of rust, cracks, chips, bent areas, or missing pieces.

b. Check jointed instruments to assure free movement, full closure, and locking of ratchets and to assure that the teeth or serrations meet properly.

c. Check sharp or pointed instruments for sharp edges or points and, if applicable, proper closure of cutting edges.

d. Spinal needles and others requiring a stylet should be sorted according to type, gauge, and length. The needle and its corresponding stylet should be straight, sharp, and free from hooks and burrs.

e. Sort suture needles according to type and size and inspect them for burrs, hooks, dullness or distortion from normal shape.

f. Endoscopy instruments should be checked for scratches or other defects that may appear on the metal. Inspect both the outside and inside of the cannula. Check to assure that the lens cover is not cracked or cloudy and that the bulbs are working. The connectors should be tight and there should be no breaks in the wire insulation.

g. Linen should be inspected for tears, holes, thin or frayed areas, ripped seams, missing ties or belts, stains or other defects.

h. Local policy should be followed regarding repair, replacement, or disposal of items which are not serviceable in their present condition.

16. Packaging for Sterilization. Most items must be packaged before they are sterilized so that they will stay sterile until they are ready for use. (This does not apply to instruments sterilized in open trays and taken directly to the operating room or articles sterilized in liquid germicides.) Several types of packaging materials are available. Paper, plastic, and fabric wrappers are commonly used, and they are not necessarily interchangeable. However, all must meet certain prerequisites:

a. The wrapping material must provide protection against contamination in handling after sterilization.

b. It must be an effective dust filter and guard against insects and vermin entering when the package is stored.

c. The wrapping material must be of known porosity and must be permeable to the sterilizing agent.

d. The wrapper must be durable enough to withstand the handling that is necessary from the time an item is wrapped, through sterilization, storage, and use.

e. The size, shape, and nature of the item to be packaged must be considered. For example, sharp or pointed items must be packed so that they cannot cut or penetrate the wrapping material.

17. Size and Density of Packages. The size and density of the package to be sterilized have a direct relationship to the time that is required for the sterilization process. Basic exposure times have been established as 30 minutes at 250° F for the gravity displacement sterilizer and 4 minutes at 270° F for the prevacuum high-temperature sterilizer. In order to assure positive steam penetration and sterilization at these times and temperatures, the dimensions of the largest package should not exceed 12 by 12 by 20 inches and 12 pounds in weight.

18. Arranging Items for Packaging. A standard method of arranging items is necessary in order to assemble a package properly. This is usually done by an indexed file-card system. The file card should describe the use, method of cleaning, contents, wrapping, sterilization, storage and stock level. An example of the suggested entries on the index file card is shown in figure 3.

a. Packages should be wrapped loosely and arranged so that the sterilizing agent will circulate freely into the center of the contents.

b. Different types of supplies, such as basins and linens, should not be included in the same package for sterilization.

c. Impermeable surfaces must be separated by a porous material.

<u>Use:</u> (State the purpose for which this set will be used.)

<u>Contents:</u> (List in detail the items contained in this set.)

<u>Wrapping:</u> (State method for wrapping set.)

<u>Sterilization:</u> (State recommended method or methods for sterilization.)

<u>Storage:</u> (State the storage area for the set, including the cabinet and shelf numbers.)

<u>Level:</u> (Give the number of sets which is considered an adequate level for operations.)

<u>Cleaning:</u> (State the recommended cleaning method or methods for items contained in set.)

Figure 3. Suggested Entries on Index File Card.

d. Box locks on instruments must be open for positive penetration by the sterilizing agent.

e. Items should be arranged in the order or sequence in which they will be used as much as possible.

19. Methods of Wrapping. There are several acceptable ways to wrap packages. The wrapper must be large enough to wrap completely around the item that is to be packaged. Linen wrappers should consist of four thicknesses (two double thicknesses). Two basic methods of wrapping packages are by the diagonal method and the straight method.

a. The diagonal (butcher wrap or envelope style) is used for small packages. Two wrappers should be used, but if only one wrapper is used, or if the second wrapper is used as part of the inner package, the item will have been wrapped in a double-thickness instead of a four-thickness wrapper.

(1) Place two wrappers of the same size, one on top of the other, on the work table with one corner toward you. Place the item to be wrapped in the center of the wrapper, parallel to the table edge.

(2) Fold the nearest corner over the item to be wrapped, then fold the same corner back to the point of the original fold.

(3) Fold the left corner over the item that is being wrapped and then fold the right corner over the item.

(4) Fold the remaining corner toward you and secure without tucking the corner.

b. The straight fold (drug store or square wrap) is used for basin sets and linen packs when sheets are used instead of a wrapper.

(1) Place the item that is to be wrapped in the center of the wrapper and square with its sides.

(2) Fold the side toward you over the top of the item that is being wrapped, and then half-fold it back toward you, making a cuff.

(3) Repeat step (2) with the other side.

(4) Fold the left side over the item that is being wrapped, tucking the ends under the outer fold.

(5) Repeat step (4) with the opposite end.

(6) Secure the package with indicator tape. A linen pack wrapped by the straight fold method is illustrated in figure 4.

20. Labeling Packages. The contents of packs, packages, sets, and fluids must be identified as the supplies are prepared. Otherwise, it would be impossible to know the contents of each pack or the type of fluid once they are all mixed together for sterilization. In addition, each must be dated when it is removed from the sterilizer.

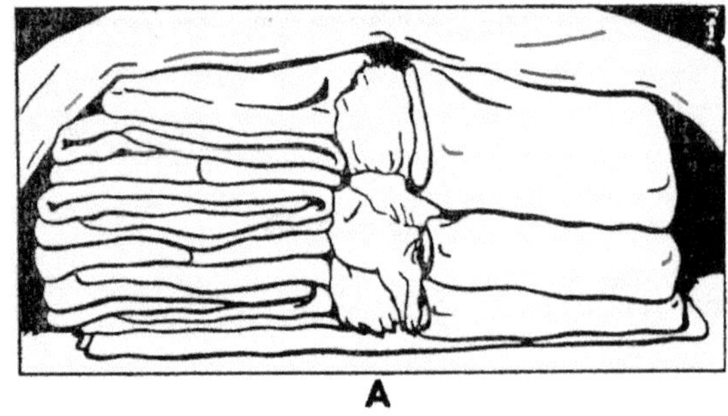

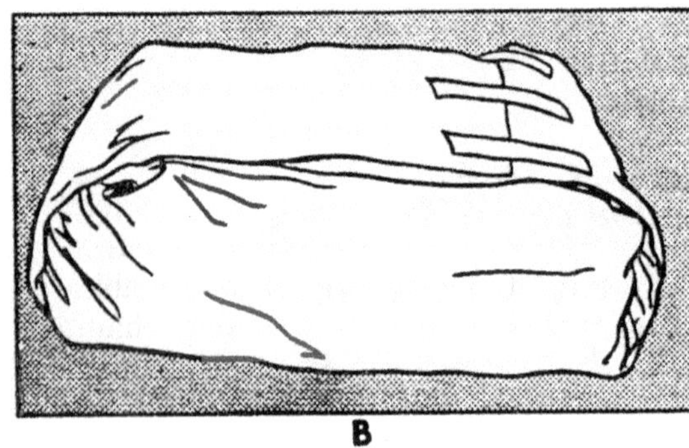

Figure 4. Linen Pack Wrapped by the Straight Fold Method.

a. Information on the label should include the name of the article and the initials of the person preparing the package. Standard nomenclature and abbreviations should be used.

b. Date the packages as they are removed from the sterilizer. (Undated packages are not considered sterile.) The date used is the date when the sterility of the item is no longer assured; that is, the date when the package must be returned for reprocessing.

SECTION D—DISINFECTION

21. Definition. Disinfection is a process which destroys or inhibits the growth of microorganisms, but which cannot be relied upon to produce sterility. Disinfection must be clearly differentiated from sterilization since disinfection may or may not destroy microorganisms, but sterilization completely destroys them.

22. Purpose of Disinfection. Disinfection is used when sterilization is not feasible. Ideally, all material that is used in the care of patients should be sterilized. However, the construction of many materials and the procedures available to sterilize by thermal methods make this impossible. In addition, chemical agents capable of producing sterilization are too toxic for use on human body surfaces.

23. Methods of Disinfection. Disinfection may be accomplished by chemical agents (germicides) or by physical means (boiling):

a. Although some chemical agents are capable of causing sterilization under specific conditions, the use of chemicals normally results only in disinfection.

b. Boiling is the least desirable method of disinfection and should be used only in an emergency or when no other suitable disinfecting agent is available. Boiling is not used for disinfection in hospitals.

24. Antisepsis. Antisepsis is the process of using a mild disinfectant to render the skin and mucous membrane as free of microorganisms as possible. In this case, the relatively weak disinfectant is called an antiseptic. Antisepsis does not produce sterility as most disinfectants capable of destroying microorganisms would also destroy the tissue. (Alcohol is an exception as it is antiseptic and germicidal in the same concentration.)

25. Classifications of Articles for Disinfection. Articles to be disinfected are divided into two general categories: (1) housekeeping, and (2) instruments. Instruments are further subdivided into critical and noncritical categories.

a. Housekeeping disinfection, as the name implies, is disinfection of floors, walls, furniture, and large equipment items.

b. Instrument disinfection is divided into critical and noncritical categories according to the risk of infection involved:

(1) Critical instruments are those used to work beneath body surface areas. This also includes other instruments or items which may be attached to the basic instrument. Instruments classified as "critical" must be sterilized prior to use.

(2) Noncritical instruments are those which do not penetrate body surface areas, so sterilization, while desirable, is not essential.

26. Basic Principles of Chemical Disinfection. Certain basic principles form the basis for all procedures involved in chemical disinfection:

a. The type and resistance of microorganisms determine the effectiveness of a chemical agent.

b. Disinfectants vary in their level of effectiveness according to the chemical agent and the manner in which it is used.

c. Other factors to consider:

(1) The solution must be of sufficient strength to be lethal to the microorganisms for which it is intended.

(2) The entire surface of the item to be disinfected must be exposed to the disinfectant.

(3) The exposure period must be accurately timed as time is important for bactericidal effect.

27. Factors Influencing the Effectiveness of Chemical Disinfection. Several factors influence the effectiveness and efficiency with which a chemical will destroy microorganisms. These factors must be considered when selecting the chemical agent and procedure to be used for disinfecting specific items.

a. All items must be absolutely clean and dry. If the item is not clean, the disinfectant cannot contact the surface and any moisture present will dilute the concentration of the chemical.

b. The number of microorganisms present also affect the performance of a disinfectant. The more microorganisms present, the longer it will take for the germicide to destroy them. This further stresses the necessity for cleaning prior to disinfecting.

c. The type of microorganisms to be dealt with are an important consideration. Most chemical disinfectants can destroy vegetative bacterial forms fairly easily; however, resistant forms, some viruses, and bacterial spores are more difficult to control.

d. The concentration of a chemical agent will determine its effectiveness as a disinfectant. A good germicide, in its use-concentration, should rapidly kill the microorganisms for which it is intended. The germicidal action of some chemical agents can be increased by increasing the concentration of the chemical.

e. Any organic substance such as blood, feces, or tissue will diminish the activity of the chemical. This is an additional reason why everything must be cleaned prior to disinfection.

f. The temperature of the solution will also influence the rate of disinfection. The rate will increase with an increase in temperature and decrease with a decrease in temperature.

28. Procedure for Disinfection. Chemical agents used for disinfection are primarily in liquid form and the articles to be disinfected should be disassembled, if possible.

a. The first step must be a thorough cleaning and drying of the items to be disinfected.

(1) Use cleaning agents selected for the type of material to be cleaned.

(2) Change the cleaning solution frequently. The kind and amount of soil will affect the length of time a cleaning agent will remain active.

(3) Apply friction to remove soil and use brushes to clean tubular instruments.

(4) After cleaning, rinse thoroughly in tap water and follow with a distilled water rinse.

(5) Heat dry items which are not heat sensitive. Place them in the steam sterilizer chamber with the steam off and the door open.

(6) Air-dry heat sensitive items by exposing them to room air.

b. Submerge the clean, dry item in the proper disinfecting solution. Start timing as soon as the item is submerged and remove it from the solution when the specified time has elapsed.

29. Properties of Frequently Used Chemical Disinfectants. The chemical selected to disinfect a specific item should be the best one available for the purpose. It must also be safe to handle and nondestructive to the materials on which it is being used. Table 1 gives recommendations for chemical disinfection and sterilization.

a. The alcohols, ethyl and isopropyl, in use-concentrations of 70 percent to 90 percent are useful as antiseptics. They are rapidly cidal to vegetative bacteria and the tubercle bacillus, but precautions must be taken as they are volatile and flammable. They will also dry and irritate the skin. The disinfecting time varies according to the material to be disinfected and the type of organisms present.

b. Formalin is the aqueous solution of formaldehyde gas. Twenty percent formalin is 8 percent formaldehyde. When diluted with alcohol, its action against the tubercle bacillus is increased. It is sporacidal if the exposure time is at least 12 hours. Formalin should be used at room temperature and loses its effectiveness below 65° F. The solution is irritating to the skin, and the fumes are irritating to the eyes and mucous membrane. Bard Parker solution is a combination of 8 percent formaldehyde and 70 percent alcohol.

c. Glutaraldehyde in a 2 percent aqueous solution (Cidex) is recommended for disinfection of cystoscopes and other lensed instruments. It will destroy tubercle bacillus within a few minutes and spores in 10 hours. The solution is toxic, but the fumes are less irritating than those of formalin.

d. Iodine in the correct concentration is high in germicidal effect and low in tissue toxicity. However, iodine is a staining agent so it is often mixed with a detergent to reduce the staining caused by the iodine. These iodine-detergent combinations are called iodophors. Wescodyne, Hi-sine, Ioclide, Betadine, and Povidone are examples of iodophors. Iodophors with 100 ppm of available iodine are effective in destroying vegetative bacteria, and in higher concentrations, 500 ppm, they are effective

Table 1. Recommendations for Chemical Disinfection and Sterilization

Objects	Disinfection: Category A Vegetative bacteria and fungi, influenza viruses.	Disinfection: Category B Category A, plus tubercle bacillus, and enteroviruses.	Sterilization: Categories A & B, plus hepatitis viruses[$], bacterial and some fungal spores.
Smooth, hard-surfaced objects	1a- 10 min. 2 - 5 min. 3 - 10 min. 4a- 10 min. 5a- 10 min. 8 - 5 min. 9 - 5 min.	1b - 15 min. 2 - 10 min. 4b - 20 min. 5b - 20 min. 8 - 15 min. 9 - 15 min.	2 - 18 hours 7 - 3 to 12 hours@ 8 - 12 hours 9 - 10 hours
Rubber tubing and catheters#	3 - 10 min. 4a- 10 min. 5a- 5 min.	4b - 20 min. 5b - 20 min. 9 - 15 min.	7 - 3 to 12 hours@
Polyethylene tubing and catheters#	1a- 10 min. 3 - 10 min. 4a- 10 min. 5 - 10 min.	1b - 15 min. 4b - 20 min. 5b - 20 min. 9 - 15 min.	2 - 12 hours 7 - 3 to 12 hours@ 8 - 12 hours 9 - 10 hours
Lensed instruments	3 - 10 min. 4a- 10 min. 5a- 10 min.	8 - 15 min. 9 - 15 min.	7 - 3 to 12 hours@ 8 - 12 hours 9 - 10 hours
Thermometers‡	1c- 10 min.	1c - 15 min.	2 - 12 hours 7 - 3 to 12 hours@ (cold cycle only) 8 - 12 hours 9 - 10 hours
Hinged instruments%	1a- 15 min. 2 - 10 min. 3 - 20 min. 4a- 20 min. 5a- 15 min. 8 - 10 min. 9 - 10 min.	1b - 20 min. 2 - 15 min. 4b - 30 min. 5b - 30 min. 8 - 20 min. 9 - 20 min.	7 - 3 to 12 hours@ 8 - 12 hours 9 - 10 hours
Inhalation anesthesia equipment	1a- 15 min. 3 - 20 min. 9 - 5 min.	1b - 20 min. 9 - 20 min.	7 - 3 to 12 hours@ 9 - 10 hours
Floors, furniture, walls, etc.	3 4a 5a 6a	4b 5b 6b	None

KEY TO AGENTS APPEARING IN TABLE

1a. Ethyl or isopropyl alcohol* (70-90%)
1b. Ethyl alcohol (70-90%)
1c. 1a. + 0.2% iodine
2. Formaldehyde (8%) + alcohol (70%) solution*
3. Quaternary ammonium solutions* (1:500aq.)
4a. Iodophor - 100 ppm available iodine*
4b. Iodophor - 500 ppm available iodine*
5a. Phenolic solutions (1% aq.)*
5b. Phenolic solutions (2% aq.)*
6a. Sodium hypochlorite, 2000 ppm
6b. Sodium hypochlorite (1%)
7. Ethylene oxide gas
8. Aqueous formalin (20%)
9. Activated glutaraldehyde (2% aq.)

* 0.2% sodium nitrite should be present in alcohols, formalin, formaldehyde-alcohol, quaternary ammonium, and iodophor solutions to prevent corrosion; and 0.5% sodium bicarbonate should be present in phenolic solutions to prevent corrosion.

$ Very little direct observation has been possible.

\# Be certain tubing is completely filled.

‡ Thermometers must be thoroughly wiped, preferably with soap and water, before disinfection or sterilization. Alcohol-iodine solutions will remove markings on poor-grade thermometers.

@ Depending upon procedure used, more rapidly cidal for category A and B microorganism.

% Must first be cleansed grossly free of organic salt.

Germicidal Agent	*Chemical Base*
Phenol or Carbolic Acid	Creosol
Hexachlorophine	Chlorinated Phenolic
Benzalkonium Chloride (Zephiran)	Quaternary Ammonium
Isopropyl Alcohol	Isopropyl Alcohol
Bard-Parker Solution	Formaldehyde
Staphene and Vesphene	Phenol
Wescodyne	Idophor
Cidex	Glutaraldehyde

against the tubercle bacillus. Iodophors are frequently used as antiseptics because they rapidly degerm the skin and are relatively nontoxic. For some procedures, it is advantageous to use an iodine-alcohol disinfectant. A 1- to 2-percent iodine in 70 percent alcohol is a good antiseptic, and 2 percent iodine in 70 percent to 90 percent alcohol may be used to disinfect thermometers. Iodine solutions are corrosive and 0.2 percent sodium nitrite should be present in the solution to prevent corrosion.

e. Phenol (carbolic acid) is a solution of phenol and phenol derivatives (Creosols). Phenol, as such, is rarely used as a disinfectant. However, many compounds are derived from phenol. Staphene, O-syl, and San Pheno are examples of one percent aqueous phenolic solutions and Vesphine, Tergisyl, and Di-Crobe are two percent phenolic solutions. In the proper concentration these solutions are effective against vegetative bacteria and tubercle bacillus, but they are not effective against spores. These agents in a two percent solution are the agent of choice when dealing with fecal contamination (*E. coli*). Phenolic compounds are stable and remain active after mild heating or prolonged drying. A dry surface previously treated with a phenolic compound, which becomes moist again will become bactericidal. Phenolic compounds irritate the skin and are corrosive. 0.5 percent sodium bicarbonate should be present in phenolic compounds to lessen corrosion.

f. Some of the synthetic cationic detergents containing quaternary ammonium compounds have some germicidal activity. The "quats," in the proper concentrations, are effective in destroying vegetative bacteria but the length of exposure time required limits its usefulness. They are ineffective against the tubercle bacillus and spores and do not inactivate viruses. The "quats" are bland in nature. The "quats" are not good antiseptics as they are inactivated by soaps and detergents. Fabric will absorb the "quats" from a solution and rapidly dilute the concentrations. Zephiran 1:750 is the most commonly used quaternary ammonium disinfectant.

SECTION E—ASEPTIC TECHNIQUE

30. Introduction. Aseptic technique is performance characterized by precautions for constant exclusion of microorganisms. To perform an aseptic procedure means to take the precautions and follow the practices and safeguards which are necessary to create an aseptic condition. A protective barrier is created by wearing gowns, masks, and gloves. Handwashing, disinfection, and sterilization are all methods of excluding or controlling microorganisms.

31. Principles of Aseptic Technique. All personnel must be familiar with and observe the following general principles of aseptic technique:

a. An article is either sterile or nonsterile. IF THERE IS ANY DOUBT, CONSIDER IT NONSTERILE.

b. Touch only the outside of the wrapper or cover when opening a container with ungloved hands.

c. Always open sterile packages and packs away from the body.

d. Do not reach across sterile items unless you are gowned and gloved.

e. Always handle sterile articles with a sterile instrument or sterile gloves.

f. Once an article is removed from a sterile container, do not return it to that container.

g. Always put sterile articles on a dry surface.

h. Do not place sterile articles on the floor.

i. The principles of aseptic technique should be applied when creating and maintaining a sterile field.

j. Cleanliness of the entire work area is basic to sterility. Certain areas of articles are considered unsterile. Tables are sterile only at table level or on their flat working surfaces. Outer rims of the lids of containers, the edges of wrappers, and the rims of flasks are never considered sterile.

k. Once a sterile field has been created, it must be kept sterile until the operation or procedure is finished. Sterile surfaces must touch only a sterile surface. Moisture may contaminate a sterile field; for example, solution basins may spill and soak through covers or drapes. Adhere to all of the principles of aseptic technique. Avoid questionable circumstances, if there is any doubt, consider the item or action as unsterile.

32. Importance of Maintaining Aseptic Technique. Operating room personnel must be acutely aware of the necessity of maintaining aseptic technique throughout all operative procedures. The patient is the loser when aseptic technique is broken. A sterile article does not change appearance if it is touched by an unsterile article, such as a sleeve or hand. However, the item has been contaminated and is capable of transmitting infection. It is always better to replace a contaminated article or setup a new sterile field than to risk causing an infection in the patient.

CPSIA information can be obtained
at www.ICGtesting.com
Printed in the USA
LVHW061519230920
666904LV00010B/506

9 781731 825575